# PART ONE
## CATCH OF THE DAY

KPOK

OKAY NOW... YOU HOLD THE RACKET SO THE FACE IS LIKE SO...

IGNORE YOU?! BUT... BUT I WOULD NEVER...

AFTER YOU COMPLETELY IGNORED ME FOR A WHOLE YEAR, IT'S PRETTY STRANGE THAT YOU SUDDENLY DECIDE TO START COACHING ME.

THE... THE CHASE?

LOOK, WHY DON'T YOU JUST DROP THE CHARADE AND CUT TO THE CHASE.

4

# maison ikkoku 4

**STORY AND ART BY RUMIKO TAKAHASHI**

## TABLE OF CONTENTS

KPOK

CER-
TAINLY
NOT!

YOU'RE
ONLY
COACHING
ME SO YOU
CAN GRILL
ME ABOUT
KYOKO,
RIGHT?

JUST GET
ON WITH
IT!

HOWEVER,
SINCE
*YOU*
BROUGHT
IT UP...

MAD AT
YOU,
HUH?

I HAVE NO IDEA
WHAT I DID TO
MAKE HER SO
MAD AT ME.

I'M
BUSHED
!

THANKS
FOR THE
GAME!

...AND
NOW SHE
WON'T
TALK TO
ME AT
ALL!

SHE
DIDN'T
SHOW UP
FOR OUR
DATE...

I JUST
DON'T
KNOW
WHAT'S
GOING
ON.

6

THAT WAS TOTALLY UNNECESSARY!

TALK ABOUT BRUTAL!

WOW.

HMPH!!

...

...

I'M TALKING ABOUT *YOU*, MRS. ICHINOSE!

IT SURE WAS — DID YOU *HEAR* HER?

OH, YEAH?

GODAI IS, TOO.

YOU'RE NOT THE ONLY ONE GETTING THE DEEP FREEZE.

OH, QUIT YOUR WHINING.

MORE AND MORE...

...I'M HAVING A HARD TIME UNDERSTANDING KYOKO.

BUT JEEZ, SHE SEES MITAKA ALL THE TIME!

...I GUESS SHE DOESN'T LIKE ME SEEING KOZUE.

THAT'S KIND OF SELF-CENTERED, ISN'T IT?

I CAN'T THINK OF ANY OTHER REASON FOR IT, SO...

HECK, SHE HASN'T EVEN *TALKED* TO ME FOR A WHILE.

...BUT SHE *STILL* GETS ALL BENT OUTTA SHAPE OVER ME HANGING OUT WITH KOZUE.

NOT VERY DAMN FAIR!

BESIDES, IT'S NOT LIKE I'VE REALLY GOTTEN ANYWHERE WITH HER...

NOW I'M STARTING TO GET *MAD.*

UH-OH...

I'M NOT A TOY FOR YOU TO PLAY WITH, KYOKO!!

DAMN IT!

...NOBODY WAS LISTENING.

I... I SURE HOPE...

...

...THIS IS JUST GOING TO GET WORSE IF I SIT HERE BROODING.

WELL...

EH?

OH, GOOD – I THOUGHT EVERYONE MIGHT BE OUT.

MAY AS WELL SHOW UP FOR AFTERNOON CLASSES.

WHAT THE HECK...

AW, IT'S NOT A VERY IMPORTANT CLASS.

THANK YOU, BUT WEREN'T YOU ON YOUR WAY TO CLASS?

DO YOU KNOW WHERE SHE MIGHT BE?

Y-YOU'RE KYOKO'S MOTHER!!

M-MY NAME IS YUSAKU GODAI, MA'AM.

SAY, YOUNG MAN...

I SHOULD BE NICE TO HER. IT'LL PAY OFF EVENTUALLY...

HM?

WOULD YOU HAPPEN TO KNOW IF MY DAUGHTER HAS ANYONE SHE'S INTERESTED IN?

THAT'S... UH... KINDA HARD TO SAY...

WELL, UH...

WELL, FOR INSTANCE, HAVE YOU SEEN HER GOING OUT WITH ANYONE?

I MEAN, YOU MUST KNOW SOMETHING SINCE YOU LIVE AT MAISON IKKOKU.

THAT'S ALL FOR TODAY, CLASS.

*I'M A MAN!*

IF THERE WERE AT LEAST *SOME* MEN IN HER LIFE, I MIGHT BE ABLE TO RELAX.

THEY SAY THE HOTTER THE FIGHTING, THE HOTTER THE LOVE.

DOES IT LOOK LIKE THEY'RE ARGUING?

HE'S THE COACH OF OUR TENNIS CLUB.

WHO... IS... *THAT?*

OH, YEAH. THEY GO OUT ALL THE TIME.

HE'S EVEN PRO-POSED TO HER!

EXCUSE ME... IS... MY DAUGHTER SEEING THAT YOUNG MAN?

OH!

OH, **WELL** THEN. I SUPPOSE IT'S FINE FOR YOU TO PAW WOMEN YOU DON'T EVEN **KNOW**.

BUT KYOKO, I DON'T EVEN **KNOW** HER!

I DID INDEED.

YOU... SAW THAT?

THAT'S QUITE ALL RIGHT. YOU DON'T NEED TO MAKE UP AN EXCUSE.

IT... ER...

WELL... UH...

CAN YOU NOW?

NO, I... LOOK, I CAN EXPLAIN EVERY- THING...

14

16

SEPIA
REALLY? FOR A WHOLE YEAR ALREADY?
I'M READY TO MAKE A REAL COMMITMENT, IF ONLY KYOKO WOULD GIVE ME THE OKAY...
WHAT ARE YOU ALL GRUMPY ABOUT?
WHY AM I EVEN HERE?
BUT DON'T YOU FIND MY DAUGHTER DIFFICULT TO DEAL WITH SOMETIMES?
NO, NO! WELL, MAYBE... AT TIMES....
......
SO WHAT WERE YOU TWO FIGHTING ABOUT TODAY?
WELL, IT'S... UH...
ANOTHER WOMAN, I BET!
IT IS *NOT!*
WHY WOULD YOU-
AW, C'MON... YOU SURE LOOK LIKE THE TYPE.
YOU KNOW...
...YOU SHOULDN'T JUDGE A BOOK BY ITS COVER.

OH, ABSOLUTELY!

YOU BELIEVE ME, DON'T YOU, MA'AM?

HEAVENS, NO! IT DOESN'T MATTER ANYMORE!

SO THERE'S NO PROBLEM WITH HER STAYING ON AS THE MANAGER?

HAD I KNOWN ABOUT THIS SOONER, I WOULDN'T HAVE HAD TO TRY AND FORCE KYOKO TO QUIT HER JOB.

OH, I'M *SO* RELIEVED!

SURE — THIS IS JUST *GREAT* NEWS.

GREAT NEWS, EH, GODAI?

*NOW* WHAT DO YOU WANT?!

MOM ...?

RRIINNGG

18

DO AS YOU WISH.

...I WON'T BE TRYING TO GET YOU TO QUIT YOUR JOB ANYMORE.

?

NOW, DEAR, DON'T BE SO DEFENSIVE.

NOTHING, DEAR. NOTHING.

WHAT ARE YOU UP TO, MOTHER?!

I KNOW WE'VE HAD OUR DIFFERENCES LATELY, BUT...

AFTER ALL, YOU'RE AN ADULT NOW — IT REALLY ISN'T OUR PLACE TO TELL YOU WHAT TO DO.

LIKE WHAT?

I DON'T LIKE IT.

WHAT IN THE WORLD...?

Ching

YOU HAVEN'T EVEN *MET* HIM YET!

THAT COACH WHAT'S-HIS-NAME.

SOUNDS LIKE SOUR GRAPES TO ME.

HE'S PROBABLY RUNNING AROUND WITH A DOZEN WOMEN.

THAT'S THE PART I DON'T LIKE.

AND HE'S A *HUNK.*

THERE'S NO ROOM FOR COMPLAINT—

—ECONOMICALLY, EDUCATIONALLY, OR PERSONALITY-WISE.

THEN WHAT KIND OF MAN *WOULD* YOU AGREE WITH?!

I'VE JUST GOT KYOKO'S BEST INTERESTS IN MIND, THAT'S ALL!

IF YOU REMEMBER, *YOU* HAD A LOT TO SAY BACK THEN TOO!

EVEN WHEN SHE MARRIED THAT WONDERFUL SOICHIRO, YOU COMPLAINED ABOUT HIS AGE AND ANYTHING ELSE YOU COULD THINK OF!!

......

WELL, I'M SURE KYOKO IS ALL FOR IT!

*YOU'RE* NOT THE ONE GETTING MARRIED.

HE'S THE CATCH OF THE DAY, IF YOU ASK ME.

WELL, I HIGHLY APPROVE THIS TIME!

...... ......

THANKS FOR TAKING ME ALL THE WAY HERE.

NO PROBLEM... I WASN'T DOING ANYTHING, ANYWAY.

PRACTICE ...?

WHAT TIME DOES PRACTICE START?

ER...

OH, WELL...

IS THAT A FACT...

...

THEY DON'T PRACTICE ON SATURDAYS.

SUN

MITAKA?

YOU KNOW SOME GUY NAMED MITAKA?

WELL, YEAH... SORT OF.

YES?

CALL ME YUSAKU.

SAY, KID...

22

WELL...

IT'S KINDA HARD TO SAY...

SO... WHAT DOES KYOKO THINK ABOUT ALL THIS?

REALLY?

I JUST DON'T LIKE THE FACT THAT HE'S SUPPOSED TO BE A REAL LADY-KILLER...

BUT I'M *NOT* AN "OUTSIDER"!

LOOKING AT IT FROM AN OUTSIDER'S POINT OF VIEW, YOU THINK THIS MITAKA GUY CAN MAKE MY KYOKO HAPPY?

THOSE "GQ" TYPES IN GENERAL ARE, WELL...

I THINK I CAN UNDERSTAND HOW YOU FEEL.

YOU THINK SO, TOO?

OH, YEAH... I AGREE...

I MEAN, IF HE'S GOT A LOT OF LADY FRIENDS, IT MIGHT BE HARD ON KYOKO.

YOU CAN CALL ME YUSAKU, MR. CHIGUSA!

YOU REALLY THINK SO, KID? LOOKING AT IT FROM THE POINT OF VIEW OF A DISPASSIONATE THIRD PARTY?

HUH?

THE ANSWER IS *NO!*

YOU'RE SO NAÏVE.

**DAMN RIGHT!**

GLUG GLUG

THUD

I'M NOT LETTING *ANYONE* HAVE MY KYOKO AGAIN!

GULP

WHAT *ARE* YOU DOING HERE?

OH, DADDY...

AND WHY ARE YOU OUT DRINKING WITH YUSAKU?

MY FATHER?

WHAT?

HE SAYS HE'S NOT GOING TO MOVE UNTIL YOU SHOW UP.

YEAH...

RRIINNGG

OH... YUSAKU?

HELLO?

SAY... HAVE YOU BEEN DRINKING?

## PART TWO
# TURN THE OTHER CHEEK

IS THERE SOMETHING YOU WANTED TO TALK ABOUT?

SO WHAT ABOUT KYOKO **NOW?**

I... I DON'T KNOW HOW TO SAY IT...

IT BUGS ME WHEN YOU JUST SIT THERE LIKE THAT.

...
...

...
...

YOU REALLY THINK SHE'S JEALOUS?

COULD A WOMAN GET JEALOUS ABOUT A GUY SHE DOESN'T CARE ABOUT?

WHAT **ELSE** DO YOU EVER TALK ABOUT?

AKEMI, HOW'D YOU KNOW?

YOU'VE BEEN EATING AT KOZUE'S, LIKE, TWICE A WEEK.

I MEAN, LOOK...

...
...

MAYBE SHE JUST DOESN'T LIKE *YOU*, YOU WORM.

WELL, SHE MAKES ALL THESE COMMENTS WHEN I SEE KOZUE.

BUT YOU KEEP SAYING, "THERE'S NOTHING BETWEEN US!"

EXPLOITER.

COWARD.

WISHY-WASHY

GUT-LESS.

USER.

G'NIGHT!

WORM.

VOOOM

"MAYBE SHE JUST DOESN'T LIKE YOU..."

THAT'S NICE.

WELL, I'M OFF!

IT'S TIME I FINALLY MADE MY DECISION.

29

OH! YES?

HEY, KYOKO!

...
...

BUT I LOVE SWEEPING... REALLY!

DIDN'T YOU JUST SWEEP THIS MORNING?

UM... SWEEPING?

WHAT ARE YOU DOING OUT HERE?

WHY, THANK YOU.

THOUGHT I'D BRING THE RENT EARLY.

MAYBE SHE DOESN'T COMPLETELY HATE ME.

FUNNY HOW SHE'S ALWAYS SWEEPING THE FRONT WHEN I HAVE A DATE.

I'VE GOT TO LET KOZUE KNOW WITHOUT HURTING HER.

GENTLY ...

I'VE GOT TO DO SOMETHING!

hee
hee
hee
hee

I HAVE TO TELL HER NOW!

WHAT'S WRONG, YUSAKU? YOU DON'T LOOK HAPPY.

HM? OH... REALLY?

...UM...

WELL... YOU SEE...

YES?

KOZUE, I DON'T KNOW HOW TO SAY THIS, BUT...

I HAVE TO BREAK UP WITH YOU.

BUT... WHY?

WH-WHAT?

......

I'VE BEEN THINKING ABOUT IT FOR A WHILE NOW. BUT I COULDN'T BRING MYSELF TO HURT YOU.

PLEASE! BE QUIET!

I'VE TRIED TO BE EVERYTHING FOR YOU! BUT, NOW YOU–

BUT... BUT HOW CAN YOU DO THIS? WHY?

ANSWER ME!

I'VE EVEN TOLD MY PARENTS ABOUT YOU! WHAT'S HAPPENED?!

ANYWAY, THIS BAND'S ACT IS, LIKE, SO GROSS!

...I'VE... GOTTEN ENGAGED!

THE TRUTH IS, I'VE...

DO THEY REALLY BRING A PIG'S HEAD ON STAGE?

ZIP

ZIP

32

YOU WERE *TWO-TIMING* ME?!

YOU... *WHAT* ?!

HWOOOOOO

I WON'T MAKE IT THAT *EASY*!!

I WON'T LET YOU GO!

YOU *WORM*!

HOW COULD YOU BE SO... CRUEL?

Y-YEAH, ME N-NEITHER.

JEEZ. I NEVER THOUGHT I'D SEE ANYTHING LIKE THAT.

BWAAAH!!

......

I... UH... I GUESS NOT.

COULDN'T SHE TELL HE WAS JUST USING HER?

YEAH...

JUST... HOR-RIBLE.

WHAT A HORRIBLE MAN!

I MEAN... WHO COULD?

YEAH.

I COULDN'T HANDLE THAT.

...

THAT'S IT FOR TODAY'S PRACTICE.

...

NOT YET, I'M AFRAID.

WELL...

HAVE YOU MADE UP WITH KYOKO?

YES?

HEY, COACH.

PRETTY CONFIDENT, AREN'T YOU?

I'M GOING TO GIVE KYOKO SOME TIME TO CALM DOWN.

IT'S NOT THAT I'M CONTENT, REALLY.

SO WHY DO YOU LOOK SO CONTENT?

DAMN CONFIDENT.

DOESN'T THE FACT THAT SHE'S JEALOUS OF ME SAY SOMETHING?

I'VE JUST DECIDED NOT TO HURRY.

hmph!

asics

glint

COULD YOU STOP PEEKING OVER?

HE WON'T WANT YOU FOR- EVER!

YOU'VE SURE GOT NERVE.

heh heh heh

WELL, I'LL SEE YOU LATER.

I DON'T NEED A MAN IN MY LIFE ANYMORE.

I'LL BE FINE.

OH?

...
...

YOU'RE SO STUBBORN! HOW LONG DO YOU PLAN TO BE MAD?

NOW THAT HURTS!

I'M NOT THAT KIND OF WOMAN!

THAT'S VUL- GAR?

DOESN'T YOUR **BODY** EVER CRY OUT FOR A MAN?

DON'T BE SO VUL- GAR!

36

NO, NO, IT WON'T GO LIKE THAT. I'M SURE OF IT.

HOW COULD YOU LIE TO ME?!

-SIGH-

...WHY SHOULD IT BE SO COMPLICATED?

EVEN IF I DO BREAK UP WITH HER...

I NEVER EVEN KISSED HER!

YOU'RE NOT EATING WITH THE NANAO FAMILY TONIGHT?

HI... I'M HOME.

DINNER-TIME, MR. SOICHIRO.

...

I'VE GOT TO STOP EATING OVER THERE.

SHE'S RIGHT

CAN YOU BELIEVE HIM, MR. SOICHIRO?

DIDN'T EVEN ANSWER!

WELL!

KIKO

nnnn?

...
...

nnnn?

WHY DOESN'T HE JUST PICK A REGULAR NIGHT OF THE WEEK TO GO OVER THERE?

...
...

IS IT KOZUE?

PROBABLY ANOTHER DINNER INVITATION.

YUSAKU! TELEPHONE!

THE NEXT DAY...

UH-HUH.

HI.

hsst

THANKS, BUT I'LL HAVE TO BEG OFF TONIGHT.

WHY DO I BOTHER EVEN THINKING ABOUT THAT HOPELESS...

YEAH

SURE.

SEE...

I FEEL LIKE I'VE BEEN MOOCHING OFF YOU.

TOMORROW?

SORRY, BUT I DON'T THINK SO.

...
...

I JUST NEED TO STRAIGHTEN OUT MY PRIORITIES, YOU KNOW?

NO, THERE'S NO HEAVY MEANING HERE.

40

UM... 'SCUSE ME.

BUT HERE'S THE RENT.

SORRY I'M LATE.

THANKS.

KYOKO?

YES?

NOK NOK

WHAT IS IT?

...
...

YEAH?

YUSAKU?

BOY, WAS HE COLD!

...
...

IT'S NOT IMPORTANT.

UM..

OKAY, WHATEVER.

SEE YOU.

41

I TURNED DOWN A FREE MEAL!

...
...

IT IS *NOT*!

IT'S BECAUSE OF THE WAY YOU TREAT HIM.

MAYBE I'LL TAKE THAT LOAN FROM MY FRIEND.

*grrrowl*

OH, WELL.

AS OF TOMORROW, MY FOOD BUDGET IS...

MAYBE I SHOULD HAVE ASKED FOR A DELAY ON THE RENT.

...
...

GOOD MORNING.

I'M STARVING!

CAN HE REALLY BE THAT UPSET WITH ME?

HE LOOKS MISERABLE.

SEE YA.

43

AKEMI?

HI THERE.

WELL, HI KYOKO!

OH, YEAH, YOU'RE GIVING UP MEN.

WELL... NO!

YOU GOT A DATE?

UH-HUH.

IS THIS YOUR DAY OFF?

THAT'S WHAT I SAID.

I'M DOING NOTHING OF THE KIND.

WELL, AREN'T YOU?

COULD YOU PLEASE NOT PUT IT QUITE THAT WAY?

DON'T WORRY ABOUT IT. I KNOW WHAT YOU MEAN.

I DON'T MEAN I'M NOT... I MEAN...

44

WHY DO YOU SOUND SO HAPPY?

OH! YOU'RE HAVING A FIGHT!

NONE! I HARDLY EVEN SPEAK TO HIM.

SO, NO MORE DATES WITH THE TENNIS COACH, HUH?

BECAUSE I *AM*!

NOT REALLY. HE DOESN'T TRY TO TALK TO ME EITHER.

ISN'T IT KINDA AWKWARD?

I GO THERE TO BRUSH UP ON MY TENNIS, NOT TO SEE SHUN!

THEN WHY DO YOU STILL GO TO THE COURTS?

I SUPPOSE...

I WONDER...

CAN IT BE?

...

SO HE DOESN'T LIKE YOU ANYMORE!

BUT I'M NOT TRYING TO TIE THEM DOWN!

THE WAY YOU WON'T LET THOSE GUYS GET ANYWHERE BUT YOU STILL TRY TO TIE 'EM DOWN.

IF YOU MUST KNOW, I THINK YOU'RE BEING SELFISH.

YOU... YOU DO?

PLAYING MISS INNOCENT.

THAT'S EVEN SCARIER. DOING IT WITHOUT TRYING!

AKEMI, WOULD YOU *PLEASE* NOT PUT IT THAT WAY!

HE'S GOT TO. HE'S NOT GETTING ANYTHING OFF YOU.

MAYBE HE HAS ANOTHER WOMAN IN HIS LIFE.

POOR SHUN! IN THE PRIME OF HIS MANHOOD, YET!

*I'D* GIVE HIM WHAT HE NEEDS!

WHY ALL THIS FUSS ABOUT SHUN AND YUSAKU?

SO WHAT IF I'VE BEEN A LITTLE COOL TO THEM?

SLIPPIN' THE BUCKS RIGHT INTO MY ACCOUNT! I CAN EAT AGAIN!

THANK GOD FOR PARENTS!

GREAT TO BE BACK!

WELCOME HOME!

IT'S SO NICE TO SEE A SMILE ON THAT FACE AGAIN!

AND SO THE TRIANGLE IS REPAIRED...

heh heh

heh heh

# PART THREE
# SOICHIRO TURNS
# AROUND

MY GRANDPA.

WHO TOLD YOU THAT?!

IS IT TRUE AUNTIE KYOKO'S GETTING REMARRIED?

TOK

UM...

IF THE SPEAKER'S CHANGING THE...

TO **WHOM**?!

大福帳

H-HERE I AM!

I HOPE IT'S OKAY!

I'M OPENING THE DOOR!

SO IF HE'S CHANGING THE SUBJECT...

I GET IT.

**NOK NOK**

WHO'S SHE SUPPOSED TO BE MARRYING?!

DON'T CHANGE THE SUBJECT!

ANSWER ME, IKUKO!

I'M COMING IN!

KLOP!
KLOP!
KLOP! KLIK

I AM!

ARE YOU PAYING ATTENTION, IKUKO?

SINCE YUSAKU'S SPENDING THIS EXTRA TIME...

OKAY, GRANDPA WAS SAYING...

SO WHAT ABOUT HER REMARRYING, HUH?

...THEN SHE WON'T BE UNCLE SOICHIRO'S WIFE ANYMORE...

IF AUNTIE KYOKO GETS REMARRIED...

...HOW MAYBE IT'S TIME SHE GETS MARRIED AGAIN. 'CAUSE HE'S GETTING WORRIED ABOUT HER.

WHAT WOULD SHE BE THEN?

THE WORD'S "UN-RELATED."

...SO SHE WON'T BE ABLE TO BE MY AUNT!

OH, JEEZ.

IS THAT ALL?

52

HOW COME?

I DON'T THINK YOU'VE GOTTA WORRY...

...MUCH.

...

...

I DON'T WANT THAT TO HAPPEN.

GREAT!

I THINK IT'LL BE A WHILE.

WELL...

WHEN YOU LIVE IN THE SAME BUILDING, YOU GET TO KNOW PEOPLE.

AUNTIE...

DID YOU GET ALL YOUR QUESTIONS ANSWERED?

UH-HUH.

WHAT?

DO YOU STILL REMEMBER THINGS ABOUT UNCLE SOICHIRO?

...RIGHT HERE IN MY CHEST...

IT USED TO BE, WHENEVER I THOUGHT OF HIM...

BUT SOMEHOW... IT DOESN'T HURT MUCH ANYMORE.

?

YES. I REMEMBER.

YOU KNOW, I'VE ALWAYS WANTED TO ASK YOU...

...IT WAS PHYSICALLY PAINFUL.

WOW...

...IT WOULD BECOME SO TIGHT...

IT JUST HAPPENED.

WHY DID YOU GIVE UNCLE SOICHIRO'S NAME TO THE DOG?

54

HM?

OH, SOICHIRO!

HE'S FILTHY. HE MUST BE A STRAY.

HE FOLLOWED ME FROM THE STATION.

WHO'S THE DOG?

JUST IGNORE HIM.

HE ISN'T GOING AWAY AS IT IS!

SOONER OR LATER HE'LL LEAVE.

SHOULD I GIVE HIM SOME?

I GUESS HE WANTS MY YAKITORI.

IF YOU DO THAT, HE'LL NEVER GO AWAY!

THAT'S YOUR NAME, DON'T YOU UNDERSTAND?

SNOWY.

BOY, YOU'VE GOT SOME NERVE FOR A DOG!

AND HE'S BEEN HERE EVER SINCE.

BOWF!

OKAY.

DINNER'S READY, SOICHIRO.

SNOWY!

...
...

57

IS MR. SOICHIRO BACK?

WHAT'S WRONG, KEN-TARO?

A FEW DAYS LATER.

MISS MANAGER!

WELL... UH... SEE...

BUT YOU WERE THE ONE WHO TOOK HIM FOR A WALK!

WHEN I WAS AT THE RAILROAD CROSSING...

...
...

HE GOT LOST!

DING DING DING

MR. SOICHIRO! STOP!

snf snf

DING DING DING

Sniffff

ROOOOOOR

I'M SURE HE'LL COME BACK!

IT'S ALMOST DINNER-TIME!

I'LL FIND HIM!

BUT, KENTARO! WAIT!

I'M GONNA GO LOOK AGAIN!

OH, NO!

HE MUST HAVE FOLLOWED THE GRILLED CHICKEN!

I LOOKED ALL OVER, BUT...

WHEN THE TRAIN WENT BY... WELL...

...

...

WHAT AM I GONNA DO?

WHAT IF HE NEVER COMES BACK?

MR. SOICHIRO?

...

IF ANYTHING HAPPENS TO HIM...

MISS MANAGER LOVES HIM!

SHUT UP!

IT'S NOT LIKE A DOG CATCHER'S GOING TO GO AFTER THAT LUMP.

FEAR NOT. SURELY HIS BESTIAL INSTINCTS WILL LEAD HIM HOME.

YES.

STILL ...?

GOOD MORN- ING!

BUT KENTARO'S SO UPSET ABOUT IT.

I'LL SEARCH IN MY SPARE TIME.

DON'T.

IT'LL WORK OUT.

HE SHOULDN'T BE.

IT'S MR. SOICHIRO'S FAULT FOR GOING AFTER THAT YAKITORI.

GOOD MORN- ING.

OH!

LOST DOG

OLD MANGY WHITE DOG CALL (04

...
...

...DID HE HAVE TO SAY "MANGY"?

BUT...

I ALWAYS THOUGHT OF HIM AS "SHAGGY."

HE MUST REALLY FEEL TERRIBLE.

OH, KENTARO...

MR. S

A WEEK PASSES.

SUDDENLY IT FEELS HUGE.

ALWAYS THOUGHT THIS WAS A SMALL TOWN.

A BIG OLD WHITE MANGY ONE?

HEY, KIDS, HAVE YOU SEEN A STRAY DOG AROUND?

UH-UH! SORRY!

IT'S ALL RIGHT, REALLY.

PLEASE TELL POOR KENTARO NOT TO FEEL BAD.

MY KID'S SO DAMN CARELESS.

I'M REALLY SORRY.

WE'RE ALL SO WORRIED.

WHERE CAN YOU BE?

GUESS I'LL CHECK THE POUND AGAIN.

BUT I'M RUNNING OUT OF HOPE.

...
...

63

... ...

...GONE.

HE'S...

SOICHIRO ISN'T HERE ANYMORE.

OH, SOICHIRO...

HE WANTS TO NAME IT...

BUT MOM!

WOULD YOU TWO BE QUIET?!

NO, IT'S NOT! IT'S JULIE!

IT'S CAESAR!

WHERE WOULD THAT STUPID DOG GO?

NOT AT THE POUND...

"DOPEY" IS THE NAME FOR THAT MUTT!

QUIET! YOU CAN'T CALL A MANGY DOG LIKE THAT CAESAR OR JULIE!

HE BARKED 'CAUSE YOU GAVE HIM FOOD!

YOU SEE? HE BARKED WHEN I CALLED HIM DOPEY!

HERE'S YOUR DINNER, DOPEY!

BOWF

BOWF

SOICHIRO!

66

AREN'T YOU HAPPY, KYOKO?

...
...

haf haf

GO GET HER, SOICHIRO!

BOWF

...
...

I DON'T GET HER.

I THOUGHT I'D BE MAKING HER HAPPY.

THE STRANGEST THING.

BUT YUSAKU LOOKS NOTHING LIKE HIM.

IS SOMETHING WRONG?

UM... KYOKO?

WHAT?

THANK YOU VERY MUCH.

OH! UM...

68

# PART FOUR
# A BUNCH OF MUGS

WELL, I GOT THIS JOB AT A PUB—

ARE YOU IN THE AREA TO VISIT HIM?

GOOD IDEA.

IT'S ONLY FOR A WEEK OR SO, SO I FIGURED I'D JUST CAMP OUT AT HIS PLACE.

YEAH... THE BIG ONE ACROSS FROM THE STATION.

THE ONE YUSAKU'S WORKING AT?

NAW, IT'S THE WHOLE WEEK'S WORTH.

YOU MUST BE HUNGRY...

BUYING DINNER

YUP.

WELL, I FIGURE I'LL GRAB A BITE OUT, EVERY ONCE IN A WHILE.

THAT'S NOT MUCH, THEN.

SAKAMOTO, MA'AM.

YUSAKU'S FRIEND FROM COLLEGE...

SAY... YOU'RE... UM...

YES?

KYOKO, I'M—

NOT MUCH...

SO WHAT WERE YOU TALKING ABOUT?

YOU BET!

SEE YOU BACK AT THE APARTMENT.

THE GYOZA THEY MAKE HERE ARE GREAT — LOADED WITH GARLIC!

HEY, SAKAMOTO, WANNA GRAB SOME POT STICKERS?

MAN, WHAT A LADY...

WHAT ?!

I FINALLY GOT TO TALK TO YOUR APARTMENT MANAGER...

WHAT'S YOUR PROBLEM?

WELL, *THAT* BROUGHT ME BACK TO EARTH...

WHAT ARE YOU COMPLAINING ABOUT? YOU *LIVE* WITH HER!

YOU MORON! WHY DIDN'T YOU CALL ME?!

IT'S MORE LIKE TORTURE.

YOU REALLY THINK SO?

LUCKY SLOB...

JUST 'CAUSE SHE'S NEAR DOESN'T–

HAVING A BABE LIKE THAT AROUND ALL THE TIME...

MAN, YOU LUCKY SLOB...

A "WORM"?!

NOT EXACTLY!

KINDA LIKE HAVING A WORM ON A HOOK IN FRONT OF YOU ALL THE TIME?

...

...

THE BUSTED ONES ARE YOURS.

...AND I HAVE TO RESIST THE SUDDEN URGE TO GRAB HER AND SQUEEZE HER TIGHT.

KRUNCH

WHEN WE TALK, STANDING CLOSE... THE AIR IS FILLED WITH HER HEAVENLY SCENT...

74

MAN, YOU'RE LUCKY... SHE'S SO NICE.

"YOU'RE WELCOME, *TOO*," SHE SAYS...

WHAT DOES THAT MEAN, "TOO"...?

WHAT'S UP, YUSAKU?

"NICE," HUH... THAT REMINDS ME...

GREAT, GREAT!

HOW IS IT, YUSAKU?

SEEMS LIKE IT'S BEEN A LONG TIME SINCE SHE'S BEEN SO NICE TO *ME*...

IF *YOU* WEREN'T HERE, I'D AGREE!

HA HA HA

JUST "GREAT"...? IT'S THE BEST I'VE EVER HAD!

THE *DEATH* PART CAN BE ARRANGED...

GEE, YUSAKU... SOMETHING WRONG?

DAMN YOU, SAKAMOTO!

MAN, I'D *DIE* TO HAVE A WIFE LIKE YOU, KYOKO!

OH, COME ON!

WELL, HEY, THEN YOU GOTTA COME TO THE PUB!

WELL, A LITTLE BIT'S OKAY...

YOU MEAN LIQUOR?

SAY, MA'AM... YOU A DRINKER AT ALL?

OH, DON'T WORRY...

ER... I'LL PAY AS THANKS FOR DINNER.

OH, C'MON... I INSIST.

YOU DON'T OWE ME ANYTHING.

YOU COOKED DINNER FOR MY FRIEND HERE, SO NOW I OWE YOU ONE.

I MEAN, THIS IS REALLY BETWEEN YOU AND ME, RIGHT?

WELL...

OH, NO, HE WON'T! IT'S MINE!

DON'T FORGET! AND I'LL PICK UP THE TAB.

MAYBE I'LL DROP BY TOMORROW, OKAY?

...

...

I JUST DON'T LIKE GUYS MAKING PASSES AT MY MANAGER!

YOU ACT LIKE YOU OWN HER!

JEEZ...

AAHH... THAT HITS THE SPOT.

LEMME HAVE A SIP.

...!

OH, GREAT... ANOTHER PARASITE.

HEY THERE, KID!

H-HI!

AH! HOW UNFAIR!

OOPSIE... ALL GONE!

UH... THAT'S MY—

TERRIBLY DISCRIMINATORY ISN'T IT, YOUNG MAN? IT SEEMS THAT YUSAKU ONLY DISPLAYS KINDNESS TO HALF-NAKED WOMEN.

WHAT WAS THAT ALL ABOUT?

WHO KNOWS?

SEE YA TOMORROW.

GOODBYE, THEN.

ZHOOP

I'M FREE TOMORROW NIGHT.

INDEED? SO AM I.

YUSAKU, YOU TAKE TABLE 8.

SAKA-MOTO, YOU GET TABLE 2.

OH, MAN, WHAT ARE *THEY* DOING HERE?!

YOU'RE KIDDING... YOU'VE NEVER BEEN TO ONE OF THESE ROOFTOP PUBS BEFORE?

NEVER.

BWA HA HA

TABLE 8...

YESSIR!

YESSIR!

WHAT THE HELL ARE YOU WAITING FOR?! MOVE YOUR BUTT!

HEY, SAKAMOTO — SWAP TABLES WITH ME!

THIS IS BIG ENOUGH FOR *ME!*

YOU SHOULDA GOT A BIG MUG LIKE EVERYONE ELSE, KYOKO.

FAST WORK, KIDDO.

HERE Y'GO, FOLKS...

WHUD

EXCUSE ME...?

...!

MOST KIND OF YOU TO INVITE US TO SHARE IN YOUR GOOD FORTUNE.

YEAH, YUSAKU'S PAYING ANYWAY, RIGHT?

...
...

CHEERS!

LET'S HEAR IT FOR YU- SAKU!

HEY, WAIT A SEC! WHO INVITED WHOM FOR WHAT?!

I'M SURE I DON'T KNOW.

SUCK IT UP, GUYS — IT'S ALL FREE!

BETTER KEEP 'EM COMING *FAST!*

WE ACCEPT YOUR KIND OFFER.

HI GUYS! DRINK UP, DRINK UP — YUSAKU'LL KEEP 'EM COMING!

HONESTLY, I DON'T HAVE A CLUE...

SOMEHOW THINGS JUST GOT ALL MIXED UP.

LOOK, KYOKO... WHAT'S GOING ON HERE?

Y-YESSIR!

DON'T STOP AND YAK WITH THE CUSTOMERS WHEN WE'RE THIS BUSY, YOU KNUCKLEHEAD!

HEY, YUSAKU — THE BOSS WANTS YA!

BWAHAHAHA!

M-ME? NO WAY!

WHAT THE HELL ?!

YOU KNOW THEM?

ALL RIGHT, LADY!

BWA HA HA HA!

MRS. ICHINOSE, PLEASE!

HEY, YUSAKU! C'MON, FILL 'EM UP!

M... MAYBE SHE SAW IT ON MY NAME TAG?

SO HOW COME SHE KNOWS YOUR FIRST NAME?

SEZ WHO?

MAYBE, BUT YOU'RE EMBARRASSING KYOKO!

HA HA

AW, THEY LOVE IT!

C'MON GUYS, CHILL OUT. YOU'RE NOT THE ONLY PEOPLE HERE!

...AND SURE ENOUGH...!

BWA HA HA

I THOUGHT THIS MIGHT HAPPEN...

I AM NOT!

SHE'S JUST DRUNK!

LOOK! SHE'S BLUSHING!

HEE HEE

IF I'M NOT HERE TO KEEP CONTROL, THEY'LL...

BUT I CAN'T JUST GO HOME AND LEAVE YUSAKU STUCK WITH THEM.

Chug it! Chug it!

C'MON! OUR MORE PITCHERS!

IF IT'S FREE, I HAVE NO LIMIT.

HEY, KID! MORE BEER!

HA HA

BROTHER, THAT WHOLE TABLE'S OUT OF CONTROL, EH?

WHAT ABOUT *YOU*, HUH?

WHAT ARE YOU TALKIN' ABOUT?

UMM... ARE YOU ALL RIGHT, KYOKO?

YOU'VE BEEN CHOKING THEM DOWN NO PROBLEM, SO FAR...

C'MON, WHY QUIT NOW?

NONE FOR ME, PLEASH...

I... I SEE...

THEY'RE JUSHT TAKIN' ADVANTAGE OF YA, LIKE PARASHITES OR SOMETHIN'.

DID Y'SHEE THEIR *EYES*, HUH?

WOBBLE WOBBLE WOBBLE

BEER

I MEAN, ABOUT THE *BILL*.

EH?

WHAT DO YOU MEAN, ME?

I'M OKAY, JUSHT C'MON 'KAY?

LOOK, JUSHT COME WITH ME.

B- BETTER NOT STAND—

86

HUH ?!

T'NIGHT, I'M GONNA ÷HIC÷ PAY.

Y- YES ...?

PEOPLE TAKE ADVANTAGE OF YA 'CAUSE YOU'RE SHO INDECISHIVE, HUH?

Y- YES ...?

DON' GIMME THAT "I SHEE" STUFF! OOH! SOMETIMSH YOU MAKE ME *SHO MAD!*

YOU THINK *FAIRNESH* OR *MORALSH* MEAN *ANYTHIN'* TO *THOSH* PEOPLE?!

B-BUT THAT'S *NOT FAIR!* YOU'VE GOTTA MAKE THEM CHIP IN!

K- KYOKO!

(CULP!)

UMM... KYOKO... DON'T YOU THINK YOU'RE A LITTLE A DRUNK?

JUSHT LEAVE IT T'—

MY "DEAR KYOKO" ...?

YOU JUSHT LEAVE IT T' YOUR DEAR KYOKO!

WHAP

I'M JUS' A **TEENSY** BIT DRUNK.

*BWA HA HA HA*

AHH... INDEED, THE BEER TONIGHT WAS **MOST** TASTY.

ALL MINE...

HEY, YUSAKU... YOU **SURE** YOU DON'T NEED A HAND?

NO, I'M OKAY... SHE'S **MY** MANAGER, RIGHT?

OH...

YUSAKU... THE CHECK...

TSK... SOME PEOPLE REALLY SHOULDN'T DRINK!

**NOW** WHAT ARE THEY UP TO?

KYOKO, DON'T! YOU'RE --≈UGHK≈-- !!

...

...

...DON'T WORRY ABOUT IT — I PAID.

DESPITE EVERYTHING, I STILL FELT AS THOUGH WE WERE CLOSER TONIGHT THAN WE HAD BEEN IN A LONG WHILE...

I TOL' YA, I TOL' YA!

HEY... DIDN' I TELL YOU T' LEAVE IT T'**ME**?

URK!

88

# PART FIVE
# THE ONE THAT GOT AWAY

SUMMER
AMUSEMENTS;
BUT THE ONE THAT
GOT AWAY;
BREAKS MORE
THAN A NET.

A FESTIVAL, HUH...

BAM BAM BAM

THEY MUST BE PUTTING ON FESTIVALS BACK IN MY HOMETOWN, TOO...

DON'T BE AN IDIOT, YUSAKU... THE FESTIVALS HERE ARE PROBABLY BETTER, ANYWAY.

MIGHT BE NICE TO VISIT THE FOLKS, TOO.

THOSE WERE ALWAYS FUN...

91

OH, I ALMOST FORGOT...

OH, WELL... IT'S THE FIRST TIME I'VE HAD ONE OF THOSE FANTASIES IN A WHILE.

YES, I CAN SEE THAT.

AH... ER... WELL, UM... I'M HOME!

THAT'S GREAT— THANKS!

I LEFT IT IN FRONT OF YOUR DOOR.

YOU GOT A BIG PARCEL FROM YOUR PARENTS.

WHOOSH

I NOTICED MR. YOTSUYA HANGING AROUND IT, THOUGH....

AH, MR. GODAI.

HEY!!

...
...

SNIK

BULL!

YOU HAVE COME AT A MOST FORTUITOUS MOMENT INDEED. ALTHOUGH I GREATLY WISHED TO OPEN THIS FINE PARCEL, I WAS VALIANTLY RESISTING THE URGE UNTIL YOU RETURNED.

92

HEY!! AND SO...

STUFF STUFF

WHAT A MAGNIFICENT SIGHT... ALL THIS FINE FOOD...

I CAN DO THIS WITHOUT *YOUR* HELP, YOU MOOCHER.

... ...

HOW COLD-HEARTED!

LOOKS LIKE IT.

A SUMMER KIMONO, YES?

I'LL CALL YOU WHEN I GET SOME NEW SADNESS.

ALL THESE YEARS, WE'VE SHARED SO MANY THINGS... JOY AND SADNESS...

YOUR FREQUENT DONATIONS ARE MUCH APPRECIATED.

HERE'S A CAN OF PEACHES, SO BUG OFF, OKAY?

WELL, YOU'RE *NOT* GETTING THIS *ONE!!!*

AS YOU WILL OBSERVE, THIS ONE OF MINE IS QUITE OLD...

MAN, I'M POOPED.

I CAN WEAR IT AND —

THIS IS GREAT...

"Dear Yusaku — We figured you probably wouldn't make it back home this summer, so we sent this parcel.

This yukata was handmade for you by Grandma, so wear it at least once, okay?

Love, your Mom.

YES?

NOK NOK

GOOD QUESTION...

SAY... ARE YOU GOING TO WEAR A YUKATA TO THE FESTIVAL?

I WILL BE GOING TO THE FESTIVAL, OF COURSE... AS A REPRESENTATIVE OF THIS APARTMENT BUILDING.

YEAH, MY GRANDMA MADE IT FOR ME.

OH, A YUKATA!

HEY, A FAN FOR THE LANTERN FESTIVAL DANCE!

UM... SOMEONE FROM THE LOCAL YOUTH ORGANIZATION DROPPED THESE BY.

THANK YOU, GRANDMA!

*YAHOO, YAHOO! ALL RIGHT!*

TAP TAP TAP TAP

*SLAM*

...

YEAH, MIGHT AS WELL! GREAT!

MIGHT AS WELL WEAR ONE, *HMM?*

OH, YUSAKU...

KYOKO...

PIYO

IT SEEMS NOTHING AT ALL HAS CHANGED IN THE PAST YEAR.

...

WHY, YUSAKU! I NEVER REALIZED WHAT A HANDSOME MAN YOU ARE!

AH, KYOKO... HOW RADIANT YOU LOOK THIS EVENING.

*chirup chirup chirup*

KTINGG
TINGG

WELL, I'M NOT VERY...

C'MON, SHUN — WIN ONE FOR ME!

HEY, YOU'RE PRETTY GOOD AT THAT.

ONE LITTLE FISHY, TWO LITTLE FISHIES...

AW, C'MON — SIT DOWN RIGHT HERE!

ONE HUNDRED YEN PER CHANCE, SIR.

SPLSH SPLSH

SHKK

MAY AS WELL TRY FOR THE BIGGEST ONE, THEN...

98

C'MON, KID — DON'T BE MEAN!

BUT IF YOU GO AFTER THE BIG ONES AND MISS, YOU HAVE A GOOD EXCUSE FOR IT, HUH?

BETTER TRY FOR THE SMALL ONES, EH?

SO MUCH FOR THAT.

WHOOPS, NO GO!

ME TOO.

I'VE HEARD OF SUCH PEOPLE.

YEAH, I'VE ALWAYS HAD A KNACK FOR THIS — THEY USED TO CALL ME THE "FESTIVAL FISHERMAN"...

splsh splsh

WOW, YUSAKU... YOU REALLY *ARE* AN EXPERT!

I'LL SPLIT THE TAKE WITH YOU, KYOKO.

I DON'T WANT TO HEAR ABOUT IT.

WHAT'S WRONG — ALREADY DONE FOR THE EVENING?

SEEMS LIKE THERE'S ONE IN EVERY CROWD, EH?

YEAH, EVEN IF THEY'RE LOUSY AT EVERYTHING ELSE, AT LEAST THEY DO *SOMETHING* WELL.

IDIOT SAVANTS INCREDIBLY SKILLED WITH THE LIKES OF YO-YOS AND FRISBEES, AND ITEMS WHICH HAVE NO BEARING ON REAL LIFE.

bwa ha ha

shkk

YEAH, RIGHT.

TOO BAD "FESTIVAL FISHING" AIN'T A PRO SPORT, EH, KID?

HERE YOU GO.

WOW, THANK YOU!

LET'S ALL GO.

I THINK I'M GOING TO GO WATCH THE LANTERN DANCE.

TOOO-KYO ONNN-DO

oooh!

aaah!

100

KOZUE!

YUUU-SAKU!

WHOOF!

HEY... WHERE'S EVERYONE ELSE?

GREAT! I THOUGHT I'D LOSE YOU FOR SURE!

GOOD IDEA.

KINDA HOT HERE...

LET'S GO DOWN BY THE RIVER.

YEAH...

LOOKS LIKE WE ALL GOT SEPARATED.

KATAK KATAK

AHH — THE BREEZE FEELS WONDERFUL.

101

WHSSHH

HMM...

bink
bink

SHE'S PRETTY CUTE, WHEN I REALLY LOOK AT HER.

HOLD IT, PAL.

NO POINT STARTING SOMETHING.

...NOBODY AROUND BUT OTHER COUPLES...

ON THE OTHER HAND...

NO, NO, NOT AT ALL. IT'S A LITTLE "HOT AND HEAVY" AROUND HERE FOR ME, ANYWAY.

UMM... WOULD YOU MIND TERRIBLY IF WE WENT SOMEWHERE ELSE?

GOOD QUESTION.

I WONDER WHERE THE OTHERS ENDED UP...

LOOKS QUIETER OVER THAT WAY...

THAT SWINE! HE'S LURING HER OFF INTO THE DARKNESS!

THERE'S NOBODY AROUND OVER THERE...

JUST OVER THIS WAY.

WHERE ARE WE GOING?

...
...

MAYBE *TOO* QUIET.

NICE OVER HERE... QUIET, LOTS OF TREES...

YES...

HE'S JUST NOT THAT KIND OF GUY.

NO...

I MEAN, SHUN IS A GROWN-UP... UNLIKE YUSAKU...

ON THE OTHER HAND... SHE SURE DIDN'T SEEM TO *MIND* COMING HERE WITH ME... SO MAYBE...

...SHE'LL THINK I DELIBERATELY LURED HER HERE FOR THAT.

IF I MAKE A PASS AT HER *NOW*...

THOOM DOOM BATHOOM

...
...

...
...
...

DAMN... WHAT TO DO?

AND IF I SUDDENLY SAID, "LET'S GO BACK TO THE FESTIVAL...."

IT WOULD LOOK LIKE I DIDN'T TRUST HIM.

N...
NOW
WHAT?!

NOW
WHAT...?

TUMP

...!

...
...

105

KYOKO...

AND SHE REALLY MEANS SOMETHING TO ME!

DAMN IT ALL, *NOTHING'S* EVER GOING TO HAPPEN IF I JUST SUFFER IN SILENCE!

DO YOU LIKE ME?

IF NOT, JUST TELL ME, OKAY?

B...

BUT...

...
...

...

...

WELL? DO YOU?

TELL ME AND I'LL STOP RIGHT HERE.

I...
I...
I JUST...

107

OKAY...

I PARKED MY CAR DOWN BY THE STATION, SO I'LL SAY GOODBYE HERE.

THE LANTERN DANCE WILL BE HELD ONCE MORE TOMORROW EVENING, STARTING FROM 7 P.M....

THANK YOU FOR ATTENDING OUR FESTIVAL, AND PLEASE COME AGAIN.

PLEASE DON'T WORRY ABOUT IT.

I'M SORRY ABOUT THAT —

UM...

REALLY?! THAT'S GREAT! THANKS, MR. MITAKA!

IF YOU WANT, I CAN GIVE YOU A RIDE, KOZUE.

YEAH...

WELL... SEE YOU, YUSAKU.

WHAT'S *HE* BLUSHING FOR?

I'M SURE KOZUE WOULD HAVE PREFERRED FOR *YOU* TO SEE HER HOME, YUSAKU.

YEAH, I DIDN'T SEE YOU AROUND ANYWHERE.

HEY, MR. YOTSUYA! WHAT DID YOU DO AFTER WE GOT SPLIT UP?

JUST *WHAT* WERE THEY DOING, ALL ALONE IN THAT PLACE...?

I WAS INDULGING IN A BIT OF VOYEURISM...

URK!

EEP!

LEAN CLOSE AND I WILL WHISPER...

NO KIDDIN'... ANY HOT COUPLES?

LOOK, YOU — VOYEURISM IS A *CRIME!*

I WAS TRAGICALLY DISAPPOINTED IN YOUR BEHAVIOR, YOUNG GODAI.

*YUSAKU AND KOZUE!*

DAMN IT, YOTSUYA!

WHADDA *YOU* KNOW, PERVERT?!

THE *REAL* CRIME IS TO RESIST A GIRL'S ADVANCES WHEN SHE THROWS HERSELF AT YOU IN THAT MANNER.

PRETTY SAD, KIDDO...

WELL, WELL... SO HE FROZE UP, EH?

I'D BETTER GO BUY A FISHBOWL TOMORROW.

CHINGG

splsh

...NOTHING HAPPENED.

SO...

112

...SO, LIKE Y'KNOW, HE...

...I WAS KINDA NERVOUS, BUT...

...AND THEN...

...AND LIKE THAT.

...THEN WE...

YUSAKU GODAI, ISN'T IT?

YEAH, YOU'VE GOT A BOYFRIEND, RIGHT?

SO HOW ABOUT YOU, KOZUE?

WOW...

YOU THINK?

AH, KOZUE. YOU'RE STILL SUCH A KID.

WELL, WE HAVEN'T REALLY... Y'KNOW.

THAT'S PRETTY WEIRD.

AND YOU'RE TELLING US YOU HAVEN'T DONE *ANYTHING*?

YOU GUYS HAVE BEEN DATING FOR ABOUT A YEAR, RIGHT?

MAYBE HE'S GOT... YOU KNOW... A *PROBLEM*.

"PROBLEM..."?

IT HAPPENS ALL THE TIME. YOU GET MARRIED, THEN YOU FIND OUT HE CAN'T PERFORM, AND *POW...*

D-I-V-O-R-C-E

...
...

IT'S HELL ON BOTH PEOPLE.

KOZUE, YOU'RE LOOKING AT ME KINDA FUNNY. WHAT'S UP?

UH...

......

REALLY? YOU SEEM KINDA DOWN TODAY...

OH... NOTHING.

?

SUMMER'S ALMOST OVER...

114

116

MAYBE SHE REALLY *DOES* WANT TO...

STILL... MAYBE THEY'RE RIGHT.

WELL, WELL!

IT'S JUST NOT THAT KIND OF RELATIONSHIP.

CUT IT OUT, YOU GUYS.

DID I? OKAY, THEN.

DON'T FORGET, YOU *PROMISED!*

HEY, YOU GONNA HELP ME WITH MY HOMEWORK OR WHAT?!

DOES "SOMETHING" REALLY MEAN "*DOING IT...*"?

DON'T FORGET TO REDO IT LATER IN YOUR OWN HANDWRITING.

'KAY.

OKAY.

HOW DID THE TUTORING GO?

... ...

LOOKS LIKE YUSAKU'S WRITING TO ME!

WHAT'S THIS?!

WHOA, MOM, WAIT A SEC—

LET ME SEE, THEN.

flip flip

---

**Exercise 3: Verbs:** *Words that describe actions*

Fill in the blank in each sentence with a verb
(examples: run, play, etc.)

Yoshiko: "Masao, wouldn't you like to _do it_ ?"

Masao: "Can we _do it_ there?" Masao points to a grassy meadow.

Yoshiko: "No. Let's _do it_ at my place."

Masao: "Will your parents mind if we _do it_ at your place?"

Yoshiko: "No, I _do it_ there with all my friends."

---

...... ......

KONK

YEAH, WHAT?

WHAT THE HELL IS YUSAKU THINKING ABOUT?

119

I'M SO GLAD I SAVED MYSELF FOR YOU!

OH, YUSAKU!

...DONE IT!

GASP

KYOKO...

...IS A WIDOW!

THAT MEANS SHE WAS MARRIED...

AND THAT MEANS SHE'S...

HAVE FUN!

I'M GOIN' OVER TO SAKA-MOTO'S PLACE.

I JUST DON'T KNOW WHERE TO START...

— AND SO...?

Kyoko Baby, you're so big now!

WAIT A SEC... I GOTTA GET MY HEAD STRAIGHT ON THIS.

PROBABLY. BUT DON'T GO TOO FAST.

WELL, ANYWAY, YEAH — I GUESS KOZUE WANTS TO. SEEMS LIKE IT, ANYWAY.

YOU GUYS SURE GET RIGHT TO THE POINT, DON'T YOU?

YOU STILL HAVEN'T, *HUH?*

YOU MEAN ABOUT GETTING' IT ON?

NO, NO, THAT'S NOT WHAT I MEAN.

I MEAN...

ROMANCE, THAT'S THE KEY — A NICE ROMANTIC SETTING, TO START WITH.

YEAH, IF YOU JUST, Y'KNOW, GO FOR IT, SHE'LL PROBABLY FREAK.

THAT'LL BE *NEVER!*

YOU PLANNIN' ON WAITIN' AROUND UNTIL YOUR MANAGER JUMPS ON YOU OR SOMETHING?

YOU'RE ALREADY 21.

*AHH...* I DON'T EVEN KNOW *WHAT* I MEAN!

URK!

URK!

YEAH, WHY NOT? UNLESS YOU GOT SOME KINDA *PROBLEM....*

HEY, IF KOZUE'S BEGGIN' FOR IT, WHY NOT?

"IF YOU DON'T GET IN SOME PRACTICE BEFOREHAND, SHE'LL THINK YOU'RE A TOTAL GEEK."

"YOUR MANAGER'S AN OLDER WOMAN SHE'S GOT EXPERIENCE.

...

"YOU PLANNIN' ON WAITIN' AROUND UNTIL YOUR MANAGER JUMPS ON YOU OR SOMETHING?"

YEAH... HOW LONG *SHOULD* I WAIT?

KATAK KATAK

MAYBE, BUT...

"C'MON, YUSAKU — EVEN IF YOU SLEEP WITH KOZUE, THAT DOESN'T MEAN YOU GOTTA MARRY HER OR..."

"I LOVE YOU."

OH, YUSAKU, YOU'VE MADE ME SO HAPPY!

YES, MY DEAR, I NEED SOME PRAC— ER, I MEAN—

OH, YUSAKU... I'M *SO* HAPPY YOU'RE FINALLY READY!

SO YOU'VE DONE IT AT LAST!

**WHAM**

SEE YOU LATER!

HURRY HOME, SWEETIE!

BYE-BYE, DA-DA!

I... BUT... NO, WAIT!

HALLELUJAH!

NOW THAT YOU'VE "DONE IT," OF COURSE YOU'LL MAKE AN HONEST WOMAN OF MY DAUGHTER. *HEH HEH.*

LET'S CELEBRATE!

I WONDER HOW *SHE* IS DOING...?

NOTHING'S REALLY WRONG WITH MY LIFE, AND YET...

I FEEL SO EMPTY INSIDE...

THERE'VE BEEN SO MANY PEOPLE LIVING HERE OVER THE YEARS...

OH, DEAR...

MY NAME'S GODAI... REMEMBER? I USED TO LIVE AT YOUR APARTMENT HOUSE...

AND WHO MIGHT YOU BE?

YES...

EXCUSE ME, BUT AREN'T YOU KYOKO OTONASHI?

I NEVER DID...

HAVEN'T YOU GOTTEN MARRIED?

SO YOU'RE STILL LIVING HERE ALONE AS THE MANAGER?

BUT HE LEFT THIS POOR OLD WIDOW BEHIND TO MARRY A YOUNG GIRL.

SO LONG AGO, THERE WAS A KIND AND GENTLE STUDENT THAT I LOVED...

YOU TOLD ME THAT YOU LOVED *ME*!!

YOU HEART-LESS SWINE!

WAP WAP WAP WAP

BUT OF COURSE! YUSAKU!

BUT THAT WAS *ME* — YUSAKU GODAI!

IT COULD RUIN MY WHOLE LIFE!

I JUST CAN'T!

IT'S ME.

HELLO, KOZUE?

*ulp!*

KOZUE CALLED WHILE YOU WERE OUT.

SORRY I'M BACK SO LATE.

HI YUSAKU.

YEAH... COME OVER TO MY HOUSE ABOUT LUNCHTIME, 'KAY?

TOMOR- ROW?

SO WHAT'S UP?

*AH, THERE YOU ARE!*

*THE NEXT DAY...*

HELLO ...?

TAKE OFF YOUR SHIRT.

...!

"SOMETHING TO REMEMBER..."

EVERYBODY'S GONE OUT.

WHERE ARE YOUR FOLKS?

HUH?

PUT ON THE SHIRT IN THAT BAG, OKAY?

I'LL GO OUT, THEN.

I CAN'T, I COULDN'T...

LOOK, KOZUE!

OH, SORRY.

WELL, MAYBE A LITTLE KISS...

BUT...

GREAT! LET'S GO...

...AND DO SOMETHING TO REMEMBER!

?

SO **THIS** IS YOUR BOYFRIEND!

YOU LOOK SO CUTE TOGETHER!

BLAB BLAB

...
...

**THIS** IS ALL SHE MEANS BY "SOMETHING TO REMEMBER..."?

WHAT THE HECK...?

BLAB BLAB BLAB BLAB BLAB

BUT I GOTTA ASK — WHY?

...
...

AW, DON'T WORRY ABOUT IT.

SORRY I DRAGGED YOU ALONG TODAY.

I KINDA WANTED TO SHOW YOU OFF TO MY FRIENDS, I GUESS.

...I'D FALL IN LOVE WITH YOU, KOZUE.

IF THERE WASN'T ANY KYOKO...

ANYWAY, THAT'S ALL.

HA, HA!

HEE, HEE!

KONK

REPENT

MAYBE JUST ONE KISS...

...MY DEAR KOZUE.

SURE!

COULD I SPEAK WITH YOU FOR A MOMENT, KYOKO?

OKAY, EVERYONE, THAT'S ALL FOR TODAY.

ABSOLUTELY POSITIVE. SO IS THAT A YES?

YES.

OKAY...

IT'D BE NICE IF YOU COULD GIVE ME AN ANSWER SOON...

...BUT ARE YOU SURE I'M THE RIGHT PERSON FOR YOU?

I'M SORRY...

I DON'T KNOW WHY I DIDN'T SAY YES RIGHT AWAY.

I'D PRETTY MUCH GIVEN UP, YOU KNOW...

...SINCE YOU'D MADE ME WAIT FOR SO LONG.

THAT'S GREAT!

SO, DID YOU KNOW ABOUT THIS?

THERE'S NO DOUBT ABOUT WHAT *THAT* MEANS!

DID YOU HEAR *THAT?!*

"ME? I WAS MY USUAL CLUELESS SELF..."

"I ONLY HEARD ABOUT THIS MUCH, MUCH LATER, BUT THEY SAID THAT AT THE TIME, MRS. ICHINOSE SEEMED PRETTY DEPRESSED BY THE SITUATION."

I CAN'T BELIEVE THEY'VE GOTTEN SO SERIOUS.

IT'S NEWS TO ME.

JUST WHEN YOU THINK YOU KNOW A PERSON...

I THOUGHT I WAS PRETTY CLOSE TO KYOKO. THOUGHT SHE'D TELL ME EVERYTHING.

134

135

I SEE...

GUESS THAT'S WHY I WAS SO SURPRISED JUST NOW.

......

I GUESS THAT SOMEDAY, EVERYONE WILL HAVE MOVED OUT AND BE SCATTERED TO THE WINDS.

BUT IT'S JUST KIND OF HARD TO BELIEVE THAT DAY WILL EVER COME.

ACTUALLY, BEFORE I FINALLY PASSED MY ENTRANCE EXAMS, I THOUGHT ABOUT MOVING OUT A LOT, BUT NOW...

WELL, SHE SEEMS GENUINELY PLEASED, ANYWAY.

I WONDER WHAT SHE MEANS BY THAT.

I'M REALLY GLAD TO HEAR THAT, YUSAKU.

NOW I'D NEVER CONSIDER LEAVING.

IT FEELS LIKE HOME TO ME.

I GUESS EVEN A GUY LIKE ME IS BETTER THAN NOTHING.

136

*heh* *heh*

ONCE IN A WHILE SHE'LL SAY SOMETHING LIKE THAT...

SHE'S A WICKED WOMAN.

...SOMETHING TO MAKE ME THINK SHE MIGHT REALLY CARE...

...AND SO SHE KEEPS ME HANGING ONTO MY DREAMS.

SO YOUNG YUSAKU IS IN A GOOD MOOD, IS HE?

*HAH... HOW MUCH YOU WANNA BET OUR CUTE LI'L MANAGER IS INVOLVED?*

DON'T EVEN BOTHER, AKEMI.

YOU'RE GIVIN' ME THE CREEPS WITH THAT GRIN ON YOUR FACE.

NOTHING YOU SAY COULD SPOIL MY GOOD MOOD.

JEEZ, YUSAKU, WHAT HAPPENED TO *YOU* TODAY?

I HEARD THAT—

OH, YEAH, I HEARD ABOUT IT, ALL RIGHT.

AH, YES... SPEAKING OF OUR HONORABLE MANAGER... HAVE YOU HEARD THE TRAGIC TALE FROM MRS. ICHINOSE?

C'MON YOU TWO — SPILL!

SOMETHING'S UP WITH KYOKO, ISN'T IT?

YEAH, YOU'LL JUST GET ALL BENT OUTTA SHAPE.

YOU MUST NOT LISTEN TO THIS.

ABOUT WHAT? WHAT?!

......

138

"COACH MITAKA."

YEAH, *RIGHT.* C'MON, HOW BAD CAN IT BE?

WE WERE TAKING EXTRAORDINARY MEASURES TO PROTECT YOU FROM THIS INFORMATION...

I CAN TAKE IT...

I...

HIS HEART WOULD SURELY FAIL WERE HE TO HEAR THE WHOLE STORY.

*HAH!* JUST TWO WORDS AND *LOOK* AT HIM.

Gasp Pant Wheeze

*HOLD IT!!*

GETTING MARR–

THE COACH AND THE MANAGER ARE FINALLY...

IT IS WHAT WE WOULD LIKE TO BELIEVE.

IS THERE?

I KNOW YOU GUYS – THERE'S A CATCH SOMEWHERE, ISN'T THERE?

"OH, YOU'VE ALREADY HEARD? HOW EMBARRASSING!"

AHEM... "I SAY, MS. OTONASHI – I HEARD YOU'RE GETTING MARRIED TO SHUN MITAKA."

ALAS, NO. IT IS MERELY THAT, SO FAR, THERE HAS BEEN A GREAT RELUCTANCE TO CONFIRM THE FACTS.

THEN... THEN IT'S JUST MORE OF YOUR RUMORS?

IMAGINE ME TO BE THE DIGNIFIED KYOKO OTONASHI...

ESPECIALLY IN *YOUR* CASE.

INDEED, WHAT RESPONSE COULD THERE BE?

IF SHE SAID THAT, WHAT WOULD *YOU* SAY, KID? *HUH?*

......

YOU'VE BEEN AWFULLY QUIET FOR THE LAST FEW DAYS...

UM... MRS. ICHINOSE, IS SOMETHING THE MATTER?

THERE'S JUST *GOT* TO BE SOME SORT OF MISTAKE.

IT... IT CAN'T BE.

EH?

ISN'T THERE SOMETHING... IMPORTANT... YOU'D LIKE TO TALK TO ME ABOUT?

LOOK...

OH, SHUN, HELLO!

HI, KYOKO SPEAKING.

RRIINNGG

I BETTER LEAVE — SEE YOU.

OH, GREAT!

YOU'VE DECIDED ON A WEDDING HALL? WHICH ONE?

JUST WHEN YOU THINK YOU KNOW A PERSON...

PSST

CLATTER

NO ONE TRIED TO FIND OUT THE TRUTH OF THIS RUMOR...

...THEY WERE ALL AFRAID TO.

...FIND OUT FOR MYSELF.

I MUST...

BUT I...

THANKS FOR HELPING ME OUT WITH ALL THE ARRANGEMENTS, KYOKO.

OH, DON'T WORRY ABOUT IT.

I JUST HOPE I WAS THE RIGHT CHOICE FOR YOU, THAT'S ALL.

BUT I'M SURE SHE WON'T LOOK EVEN HALF AS BEAUTIFUL AS *YOU* WOULD...

YEAH...

STILL — IT'LL ALL BE WORTH IT WHEN YOU SEE YOUR SISTER LOOKING SO BEAUTIFUL IN HER WEDDING GOWN!

I DIDN'T HAVE A CLUE WHAT TO... WEDDINGS ARE A COMPLETE MYSTERY TO ME.

YOU WERE A HUGE HELP.

WELL, THEY *CAN* BE A BIT DIFFICULT TO ARRANGE.

...

...

KANG
KANG
KANG
KANG

AND IF IT *IS* TRUE...

THEN... THEN... WHAT?

I'VE GOT TO MAKE SURE.

GOT TO HEAR IT FROM HER OWN LIPS.

YUSAKU...?

WELL, YES... I WAS WITH SHUN.

BEEN OUT SOME-WHERE?

...YOU'VE ALREADY HEARD?

OH...

...GOING TO BE A... W-WEDDING?

I-IS THERE...

GULP...

WHROO

KANG
KANG
KANG

GOODBYE FOREVER, KYOKO...

KANG KANG KANG

"BUT IT'S KIND OF HARD TO BELIEVE THAT DAY WILL EVER COME."

WHY DID YOU SAY THAT, WHEN ALL ALONG...

KANG KANG

KANG

KANG

WHY?!

EH?

148

SHKK

C'MON... YOU'RE NOT SERIOUS?

......

AND SO HE QUIETLY WITHDRAWS WITHOUT A FIGHT.

WHAT A WIMP.

LOOK, MS. OTONASHI KNEW HOW... HOW I FELT.

IF SHE KNEW AND STILL CHOSE MITAKA...

I'LL SEND A MOVING COMPANY TO PICK UP THE REST OF MY STUFF LATER.

I DON'T KNOW...

..BUT I CAN'T STAND TO BE HERE ANY LONGER, THAT'S ALL.

BUT WHEREVER WILL YOU GO?

WELL, YEAH... THAT'S TRUE, I GUESS...

...THEN WHAT POINT IS THERE IN PUTTING UP A FIGHT?

I'M HOME...

UM... ARE YOU GOING OUT?

YEAH... WAY, *WAY* OUT.

HM ...?

I... I CAN'T SAY CONGRAT-ULATIONS...

MS. OTO-NASHI...

...BUT I HOPE YOU'LL BE HAPPY.

I'M SICK OF MYSELF AND MY LIFE.

WHY ARE YOU—

YUSAKU, *WHAT* IS GOING ON HERE?!

THANKS FOR EVERY-THING... IT WAS NICE KNOWING YOU.

WHAT —?

WAIT!

...TIME TO LOOK INSIDE MY HEART.

I NEED SOME TIME ALONE...

GOODBYE!

HIS BIG EXIT KINDA FELL FLAT, HUH?

...WHEN DO YOU THINK HE'S GOING TO GET UP?

AND SO, I "KISSED" MAISON IKKOKU GOODBYE...

HE HAS SURELY DONE IT, THIS TIME.

WHAT DO YOU S'POSE HE'S GONNA DO NOW?

WHO KNOWS? BUT FOR STARTERS...

# PART EIGHT
## A SMALL SPACE

WHO, *ME?*

THIS IS AWFUL! I WONDER HOW THE FACTS GOT SO MIXED UP...

WHY ARE YOU LOOKING AT *ME* LIKE THAT?

HEY, DON'T ASK ME!

*I'M* GETTING MARRIED TO SHUN MITAKA?!

IT'S CERTAINLY NEWS TO *ME!*

OF COURSE!

OKAY... SO, LIKE THE STORY ABOUT YOU AND SHUN GETTING MARRIED IS A BUNCH OF BULL?

I JUST *CAN'T* IMAGINE HOW THIS STORY GOT SO WARPED...!

I WAS JUST HELPING HIM PICK OUT A PRESENT FOR HER, THAT'S ALL.

THE PERSON GETTING MARRIED ISN'T *ME*, IT'S SHUN'S YOUNGER SISTER!!

IT IS SAID, "WHERE THERE'S SMOKE, THERE'S FIRE."

UH... ER... DON'T WE HAVE MORE IMPORTANT THINGS TO TALK ABOUT?

YUSAKU ISN'T A *DOG*, MR. YOTSUYA!

PERHAPS HE WILL RETURN TO HIS HOME WHEN HE GETS HUNGRY...?

WITH *HIM?* NOT MUCH.

SO WHAT ARE WE GOING TO DO?

I MEAN, YUSAKU PACKED UP AND LEFT BECAUSE OF THIS MESS.

RIGHT, JUST SIGN THERE, AND THERE.

THE NEXT DAY...

CHING

I'VE GOTTA SAY, YOU'RE ONE LUCKY YOUNG MAN.

SO I FOUND A NEW PLACE RIGHT AWAY.

BY SIGNING, I TRULY SEVERED MY TIES TO MAISON IKKOKU.

YEAH...

YOU HARDLY EVER SEE ONE SO NEAR THE STATION FOR ONLY ¥20,000.

THIS APARTMENT WAS JUST LISTED THIS MORNING.

I TELL YA, KID— YOU'RE DAMN LUCKY.

FOR ONE THING, I'M THROUGH WITH WOMEN!

THIS IS MY CHANCE TO REALLY CHANGE MY LIFE... TO FIND MYSELF.

"SECOND FLOOR OF THE SUPER SPACE PACHINKO PARLOR"...

MUST BE IT.

ching ching

ching
tiktiktik
shrakkk
ching ching

HUH?

NOT LOCKED?

KCHAK

Shrakkk
ching

KREEE

GURK!

KREE

W-W-WRONG DOOR!

S-S-SORRY!!

HMM?

...?

SLAM

LESSEE... "CLOCK HILL STATION WEST, SECOND FLOOR OF THE SUPER SPACE PACHINKO PARLOR, APARTMENT 1"...

JEEZ, WHAT A SURPRISE!

159

I MEAN, I'VE ALREADY SIGNED THE LEASE AND EVERYTHING!

YOU THINK *YOU'VE* GOT A PAIN?

WELL, THEN, I GUESS IT'S YOUR PLACE NOW!

"DELAYED"?! WHAT?!

...'CAUSE MY PLANS TO MOVE HAVE BEEN KINDA DELAYED.

THAT'S A REAL PAIN...

I DON'T HAVE ANYPLACE ELSE TO GO, EITHER!

...SO I COULDN'T MOVE EVEN IF I HAD TO!

BUT I DON'T HAVE ANY MONEY...

I'VE GOT IT!

HEY!

SOUNDS LIKE WE HAVE A PROBLEM, ALL RIGHT.

160

WHAT?!

WE CAN JUST LIVE TOGETHER UNTIL I CAN SCRAPE UP ENOUGH MONEY TO MOVE!

PRETTY PLEASE? ♡ YOU'LL BE HELPING A DAMSEL IN DISTRESS!

WELL, *UH*, I DUNNO...

AW, C'MON! I'LL SPLIT THE RENT WITH YOU, OKAY?

B-BUT...

I MEAN...

BUT...

AS LONG AS I'VE GOT A PLACE TO STAY, I CAN'T COMPLAIN.

DON'T WORRY ABOUT THAT AT **ALL**, HON!

OH, NO!

...AND YOU'RE A GIRL, SO...

I'M A GUY...

WELL, UH...

ulp!

RIGHT?

AND IT'S GOING TO HELP BOTH OF US OUT, RIGHT?

I MEAN, WE'D ONLY BE "LIVING IN SIN" FOR A WEEK OR TWO.

ALL *RIGHT!*

I GUESS... IF IT'S OKAY WITH YOU...

SO, YOU GOING TO COLLEGE?

GOTTA BE SOME BEER IN HERE...

WHAT'S YOUR NAME?

HUH?

LET'S HAVE A DRINK TO CELEBRATE, OKAY?

162

...THIS REMINDS ME OF MAISON IKKOKU.

JEEZ...

UH, CHEERS.

CHEERS!

I'M *AYAKO.* PLEASED T'MEETCHA!

KANK

WHEN I FIRST MOVED IN THERE...

AS SOON AS I GET ENOUGH MONEY, I'M OUTTA HERE.

AH, WELL.

MAN, WHAT A GRUBBY LITTLE APARTMENT.

??

skritch
skritch
skritch

GREETINGS.

I AM YOTSUYA, FROM ROOM 4.

W-WHO *ARE* YOU?!

AIEE!

WHAM

CHEERS!

ALL RIGHT, A ROOM-WARMING PARTY! LET'S DRINK!

THUD THUD

......

HEY, KID, I HEAR YOU'RE A FLUNK-OUT!

THUD THUD

*THE ONLY REASON I STAYED IN THAT MADHOUSE WAS BECAUSE OF HER...*

BWA HA HA

I HAVEN'T EVEN UNPACKED YET!

WAIT! HOLD ON A DAMN SECOND!

164

DAMN IT, WHAT AM I THINKING?

THE REASON I LEFT THERE WITHOUT EVEN TAKING MY STUFF WAS TO MAKE A CLEAN BREAK.

...BECAUSE KYOKO WAS THERE.

KYOKO...

I'M... THROUGH WITH WOMEN...

BINK

YOU SEEM KINDA SAD...

SOME-THING WRONG, HON?

I'M *THROUGH* WITH WOMEN!

HEARD FROM YUSAKU?

...

NOT A WORD.

I SEE...

MAYBE...

IT'S JUST...

YOU WORRIED?

167

WELL...

SO WHAT DO YOU DO FOR A LIVING?

ER... AYAKO...

......

TODAY'S MY DAY OFF.

I WORK AT A MASSAGE PARLOR.

LET'S EAT!

SOUP'S ON!

AT A *MASSAGE PARLOR?!?*

SO SHE'S A...

HERE...

UH... THERE'S PLENTY, IF YOU WANT MORE.

I CAN'T TASTE A THING.

 YOU BET!

 TASTY...?

 WE ARE? I MEAN, SURE.

HUH?

SINCE WE'RE SPLITTING THE FOOD EXPENSES, TOO, IT'S A WASTE IF YOU DON'T EAT.

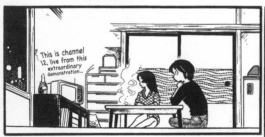 This is channel 12, live from this extraordinary demonstration...

 ...as you can see, thousands of candles...

...

MAYBE SHE'S EXPECTING ME TO...

STILL, MAYBE...

SHE SURE SEEMS RELAXED AROUND ME. MAYBE...

NAW, NO WAY.

I WONDER WHAT KIND OF GIRL SHE IS.

...for world peace...

More!

WHAT ARE YOU THINKING, YOU MORON?!

YOU JUST GOT YOUR HEART BROKEN YESTERDAY!

I'LL GET THE FUTON READY.

YOU MIND FOLDING UP THE TABLE, HON?

Y-YEAH, SURE!

GETTING LATE... TIME FOR BED, MM?

IT... IT'S FINALLY GOING TO HAPPEN...

...TO ME!

YOU MUST BE TIRED AFTER MOVING.

YOU OUGHT TO COME TO BED, TOO.

D... DON'T LOOK AT ME LIKE THAT!

YOU'RE THE ONE WHO LEFT *ME.*

YUSAKU...

...
...

MM?

SOMETHING WRONG, HON?

172

173

NOW, DEAR... DON'T BE MEAN.

I DUNNO IF I WANTS YOU LIVIN' WITH DIS YOUNG PUNK.

AND I WAS THINKING *HE* WAS ONE OF HER "CUSTOMERS."

AN' I WAS THINKIN'... JEEZ, BABY. I DON'T WANNA THINK ABOUT WHAT I WAS THINKIN'!

grind grind grind

...AND SO, HE'LL BE STAYING HERE WITH US FOR A WHILE.

......

YEAH, WULL, I GUESS SO...

AFTER ALL, HE CAN'T GO ANYWHERE ELSE RIGHT NOW.

GIVE HIM A BREAK.

AWRIGHT, GODAI— I'M GONNA LETCHA STAY HERE, SEE?

YEAH...

HEY, KID — YER NAME'S YUSAKU GODAI, HUH?

THIS IS *BACK-WARDS!*

HOLD IT!!

I'M THE ONE GIVING *THEM* A BREAK!

174

HEY, HEY!

C'MON KID... GIMME DA CASH AN' I'LL MAKE US ENOUGH TO MOVE OUT!

HUH?

HEY, PUNK... YOU GOT ANY DOUGH?

HUH.

MORE LIKE CHEAP, I BET.

ME? MONEY? I'M FLAT BROKE!

YOU GOTTA BE KIDDING!

GZ NAW GZ NAW NAW

I... I WANNA GO HOME...

⇒SNIFF⇐ KYOKO...

BETTER LUCK TOMORROW, YES?

WELL, TOO LATE NOW.

# PART NINE

# RECIPE FOR MISUNDERSTANDING

JUST SIGN HERE, MA'AM.

THANKS.

BRMBBBB

SO *NOW* WHAT DO I DO?

GUESS HE DIDN'T EVEN TELL HIS PARENTS THAT HE'D MOVED.

IT'S FOR YUSAKU...

...

VROOM

一刻館

MAISON IKKOKU

....

....

FWIP

OH, HI, MR. YOTSUYA — WHERE ARE YOU GOING?

I AM GOING OUT.

180

WHEN THE HELL ARE YOU TWO GOING TO MOVE OUT?!

SHUDDUP! WE AIN'T GOT DA DOUGH!

BE CAREFUL WITH THE DISHES, HON — THEY'LL BREAK.

CRASH CLATTER

I SAYS DAT MAKES US *EVEN!*

I GOTTA SHARE MY OWN DAMN *BED* WITCHA!

OH YEAH — THAT REMINDS ME.

WHADDA HELL YOU TALKIN' ABOUT, BOY?

"WE'LL BE OUT IN JUST A FEW DAYS..." HUH?

WHAT HAPPENED TO OUR DEAL?

CRASH CLATTER

THAT'S *YOUR* PROBLEM, NOT *MINE!*

GEE, WON'T THAT MAKE THINGS A LITTLE TIGHT HERE?

*WHAT?!*

I'M HAVING MY STUFF SHIPPED HERE TODAY.

YOU KNOW, I KIND OF HAD THE SAME FEELING MYSELF.

YOU GUYS ACT LIKE I'M YOUR KID OR SOMETHING!!

NOW, DEAR, YOU'RE DREAMING AGAIN.

I'LL DOUBLE IT FER YUH!

GIMME DAT DOUGH!

DEN WE'LL HAVE ENUFF TO *MOVE* ON, AN' YOU'LL GET SOME EXTRA, HEY?

SAY, SON... YOU GOT SOME CASH FOR TH' MOVERS,

*NOW* WHAT?

BUT IF HE COMES TO THE PARLOR, HE'LL JUST BE ANOTHER CUSTOMER, RIGHT?

DAMN IT AYAKO, YOU AIN'T GONNA... WIT DAT *KID?*

I'LL SHOW YOU A *REAL* GOOD TIME, HON.

WHAT YOU SHOULD DO IS COME TO MY MASSAGE PARLOR WITH THAT MONEY.

WHAT DO YOU MEAN, "FAMILY"?!

AND THE MONEY WOULD JUST END UP RIGHT BACK IN THE FAMILY, SO IT'S A WIN-WIN DEAL, MM?

182

I CAN STAKE OUT A CLAIM FOR SOME FLOOR SPACE.

ANYWAY, ONCE I MOVE IN MY FURNITURE...

I CAN'T BELIEVE THOSE PEOPLE!

DAMN IT ALL!

...IT'S REALLY GOODBYE, ISN'T IT?

ON THE OTHER HAND, ONCE I MOVE IT OUT OF MAISON IKKOKU...

I WONDER IF SHE'S OKAY...

KYOKO...

SPARKLE

SMILE

RRG!

CHUG CHUG CHUG

WELL, SHE'S NOT MY CONCERN ANYMORE.

BECAUSE SHE BELONGS TO THAT DAMNED MITAKA NOW.

I'M SUCH AN IDIOT...

CHUG CHUG

ANYBODY HOME...?

BUT HE LEFT ALL HIS STUFF...

...SO MAYBE...

CHUG CHUG CHUG

MAYBE I OUGHT TO JUST SEND IT BACK...

184

WHERE'S ROOM 5?

WE'RE THE MOVERS.

YES?

HUH... LOOKS LIKE THE KID *WAS* SERIOUS, AFTER ALL.

THUD THUD

......

PIYO PIYO

UMM, EXCUSE ME...

WE'RE ALL DONE HERE, MA'AM – THANKS!

WHY, THAT'S JUST THE NEXT STATION OVER.

CLOCK HILL WEST...

I... UH... SORT OF MISPLACED IT.

COULD YOU GIVE ME HIS NEW ADDRESS?

SURE, NO PROBLEM.

MAYBE... MAYBE I SHOULD HAVE JUST GIVEN IT TO THE MOVERS...

KLIK

VOOSH VROOSH

186

SIGH...

YOU DIDN'T EVEN BOTHER TO ASK *ME* ABOUT IT.

YOU DIDN'T HAVE TO GO, YOU KNOW.

SOMETIMES YOU'RE SUCH A FOOL.

HNNG... THERE'S NO ROOM, NO ROOM...

GZNAWW SNZZZ

I WONDER HOW HE'S DOING NOW...

...
...

188

RIGHT?

WELL, I CAN'T KEEP THIS FOREVER.

ASK ME IF I CARE.

IT'S ALL YER DAMN CRAP! I DIDN'T GET A WINK UH SLEEP!

DAMN IT, I AIN'T DOIN' SO GOOD TODAY.

KRAK KRIK

TOUGH LUCK — I JUST RAN OUT.

HEY, KID, GIMME SOME BALLS.

THAT'S PRETTY SAD, PAL...

MAYBE DERE'S SOME ON DA FLOOR...

YER A GODDAMN CHEAP PUNK!

AT LEAST BUY THE BALLS WITH YOUR *OWN* MONEY!

DEN GIMME SOME DOUGH.

HOW LONG AM I GOING TO HAVE TO PUT UP WITH THIS?

CHRING

ARG...

KRIK

I'M HAVING AN OFF DAY, ANYHOW.

I'M PACKING IT IN.

HEY, WHERE DA HELL'RE *YOU* GOIN'?

CHING SHRAKK

IS THAT NOT *MY* LINE?

WHAT ARE *YOU* DOING HERE?

M-MR. YOTSUYA!

NICE TO KNOW YOU HAVEN'T CHANGED.

YOUR TREAT, OF COURSE.

WOULD YOU LIKE A COFFEE?

*AHH*, I THOUGHT I WOULD NEVER AGAIN SEE YOU.

*AH*, EVERYONE HAS BEEN WELL. INDEED, IT'S AS IF YOU'D NEVER LIVED THERE.

SO... HOW HAS EVERYBODY BEEN SINCE I LEFT?

HAS... UH... HAS IT BEEN SET?

THE DATE, I MEAN.

UH...

QUITE SO.

NO KIDDING...

I WASN'T TALKING ABOUT *YOU*, DUMMY!

I FAIL TO UNDERSTAND – I HAVE NO PLANS FOR MARRIAGE.

...OF THE W-WEDDING.

OF THE...

DATE OF THE WHAT?

A...

...RUMOR?

OH, THAT.

I'M TALKING ABOUT THE WEDDING BETWEEN KYOKO AND THAT DAMN TENNIS COACH!

HUH?

FEAR NOT, THAT WAS NOTHING MORE THAN A RUMOR.

BUT DON'T CONCERN YOURSELF.

......

YOU ACTED MOST PRECIPITOUSLY, YOUNG GODAI.

IF ONLY YOU HAD LISTENED CALMLY AND RATIONALLY TO THE ENTIRE STORY...

......

EVERYONE AT MAISON IKKOKU HAS QUITE FORGOTTEN YOU, AND LIVES IN PEACE AND TRANQUILITY.

NOK NOK

KAN KAN KAN

SUPER SPACE PACHINKO...

THIS MUST BE IT.

HELLO?

SURE IS!

ER... THIS ISN'T YUSAKU GODAI'S ROOM, IS IT...?

I...

I SEE...

AYAKO... I'M LIVING HERE WITH YUSAKU.

UM, SORRY TO PRY, BUT JUST WHO ARE YOU?

...!

SHE DROPPED OFF THIS PACKAGE FOR YOU.

WHAT?! MY EX-LANDLADY WAS HERE?!

I HAVE TO APOLOGIZE TO HER FOR THIS WHOLE CRAZY MIX-UP!!

TMP TMP TMP

YES, JUST A MINUTE AGO.

...TO MOVE BACK IN!

I MIGHT STILL HAVE A CHANCE...

AHA!

196

# PART TEN
## THE LIGHT IN ROOM 5

198

SO THEN HE JUST PULLED OUT OF THE COMPETITION?

YEP!

NO KIDDING.

WHAT DO YOU MEAN, "DON'T HAVE A CLUE HOW IT GOT STARTED" ...?

WELL... *UMM...* SOMEHOW, WORD GOT AROUND THAT THE TWO OF YOU WERE GETTING MARRIED. I DON'T HAVE A CLUE HOW IT GOT STARTED, THOUGH.

WELL, WELL, WELL...

C'MON... WITH THE COACH AS HIS RIVAL?

DON'T YOU THINK IT'S DISGUSTING THAT HE GAVE UP SO EASILY?

NOT UNTIL THE BITTER END...

IF I WERE HIM, I'D *NEVER* GIVE UP...

Making his move...

There he goes...

I'M LIVING HERE WITH YUSAKU...

......

HEY, HEY — YOU KNOW SOMETHING WE DON'T?

WELL, PERSONALLY, I DON'T THINK I WAS THE REASON FOR HIM MOVING OUT.

HE... UH.

WELL, I DON'T!

Y'KNOW, I THINK YOU *DO* KNOW SOMETHING.

...I'M NOT THE ONLY WOMAN IN THE WORLD.

IT'S TRUE...

"TIME ALONE"... *HAH!*

I NEED SOME TIME ALONE... TIME TO LOOK INSIDE MY HEART.

THE REASON HE LEFT JUST LIKE THAT...

...IS BECAUSE HE HAD *THAT WOMAN* ALREADY.

HELLO, KYOKO SPEAK-ING...

UH, KYOKO, THIS IS YUSAKU.

RRIINNGG

LOOK, I'VE GOTTA TELL YOU—

HELLO? HELLO?!

AW, KYOKO, DON'T HANG UP!!

......

KCHING

YES – THEY NEVER SEEM TO GET THE MESSAGE.

SEEMS LIKE YOU'RE GETTING A LOT OF THOSE LATELY...

PRETTY MUCH.

WHAT WAS THAT? A PRANK CALL?

I *THOUGHT* SO. IT WAS WRITTEN ALL OVER YOUR FACE.

EH?!

IT'S YUSAKU, ISN'T IT?

ULP!

......

......

HE'S *NOT* ALONE!!

THAT'S NOT VERY NICE, KYOKO! HERE HE'S ALL ALONE AND DEPRESSED, AND YOU–

WHAT'S GOING ON?

YOU SURE GAVE HIM THE COLD SHOULDER.

BUT...

HE'S... NO KIDDING!

HE'S LIVING WITH SOME FLOOZY!

202

SHRAKK

CHINGG

KANG KANG

MAN, I WANNA MOVE BACK...

DUMB BROAD...

SHE DIDN'T HAVE TO HANG UP ON ME LIKE THAT.

......

HYOOOOO

WOW, SUKIYAKI!

WANT SOME DINNER?

YER BACK, *HUH?*

KLIK

SNIFF?

WHERE IN THE HECK DID THEY GET THE MONEY TO—

HEY, THIS IS GOOD MEAT.

EVERYONE NEEDS A GOOD MEAL EVERY ONCE IN A WHILE.

NOW, NOW...

LOOK, IF YOU'VE GOT THE MONEY TO SPEND ON STUFF LIKE SUKIYAKI BEEF, HURRY UP AND MOVE OUTTA HERE, WILL YA?

204

IF... IF I STAY HERE ANY LONGER...

THEY'RE GONNA SUCK ME COMPLETELY DRY!

HEY, DAT MEANS DA MORE FER ME, DAT'S WHAT I SAY!

REALLY? DON'T YOU WANT ANY MORE?

I'M GOING OUT AGAIN.

MM? WHAT'S WRONG?

(I ALREADY DID!) OW! HOT!

YUH'LL PAY FER DIS!!

**KANG KANG**

GOBBLE MUNCH GULP

HEY! HE'S EATIN' ALL DA MEAT!!

WHAT A JERK!

YEAH – I DIDN'T THINK HE HAD IT IN HIM.

WOW! YUSAKU...

...IS LIVING WITH A GIRL?!

YEAH, MUST'VE. OTHERWISE, HE'D NEVER HAVE MOVED IN WITH HER SO QUICK!

INDEED. HE MUST HAVE MAINTAINED A RELATIONSHIP WITH THAT WOMAN FOR QUITE SOME TIME.

ER, AKEMI, DEAR – YOU MIND DOING SOME WORK?

HOW COME YOU NEVER TOLD US?!

HUH? YOU MET YUSAKU? WHEN? WHERE?

IT IS MOST ODD... WHEN WE SPOKE RECENTLY, HE SAID NOTHING ABOUT SUCH A RELATIONSHIP.

I AM ASTOUNDED THAT YOU HIRED SUCH AN UNRELIABLE PERSON.

AW, AKEMI...!

BUT IT TURNS OUT HE'S A JERK JUST LIKE EVERY OTHER GUY. BREAKS MY HEART, SO I GOTTA GET SMASHED.

I SORTA SAW HIM AS A YOUNGER BROTHER...

I MEAN, HE HAD A KINDA CUTE SIDE TO HIM, *HUH?*

WHY SHOULD I?!

WOULD YOU JUST *LISTEN* TO ME?!

...THEN FACE-TO-FACE!

OKAY, IF NOT BY PHONE...

THAP THAP

I'M *NOT* INTERESTED.

LOOK, THAT WOMAN... SHE'S—

WHY, YOU-!

*YOU'RE* THE ONE RUNNING AROUND LIKE A DOG IN HEAT!!

"FOOL"...? *ME*, A FOOL?!

WOULD YOU SHUT UP AND *LISTEN* TO ME, YOU FOOL?!

AHH!

SMAK

KONK

YOU UNREASONABLE BITCH!!

YEAH...

..MAYBE.

MAYBE I'D BETTER GO THROUGH A THIRD PARTY.

I DON'T REALLY THINK IT WOULD GO LIKE THAT, BUT...

OWW...

C'MON IN!

KREEEK

ISH TH' PLAYBOY!

HEY!!

HEY!

208

SAY... YOU'RE ALL PRETTY DRUNK!

YEAH, YOU GOT A LOTTA *GUTSH* COMING 'ROUND HERE!

DON'T TRY T' ACT THE INNOSHENT WITH *ME*, SON!

"PLAY-BOY"...? W-WHAT DO YOU MEAN BY *THAT?*

fft fft

F W A P

I WILL GLADLY HEAR YOUR TALE.

I AM QUITE SOBER.

HALT, YOUNG MAN.

RUNNIN' AWAY, HUH?! COWARD!

YOU GUYS ARE USELESS.

FORGET IT, THEN.

SO SHE'S A ~HIC~ *MARRIED* WOMAN, HUH?

—AND SO SHE WAS JUST LIVING THERE WHEN I ARRIVED. SHE'S GOT A HUSBAND, TOO!

SLRP

IF YOU WILL, IN RETURN, BUY ME A DRINK OR TWO.

YESH, YESH, QUITE SO.

DO *YOU* UNDERSTAND, MR. YOTSUYA?!

I WILL RELAY THESH FACTSH TO OUR MANAGER.

DAMN IT, I TOLD YOU I'M NOT LIVING WITH HER BECAUSE I *WANT* TO!

AN' HE *LIKSH* OLDER WOMEN, TOO!

HUH... SEEMS LIKE YOU GOT A *THING* FOR MARRIED WOMEN.

I MEAN, KYOKO WASH ONCE SOMEBODY'S WIFE, EH?

SLAM

......

......

IT'D BE NICE IF YOU COULD MOVE BACK INTO MAISON IKKOKU...

WELL, I'D BETTER GET MOVING.

"WIFE."

"AYAKO."

"MASSAGE PARLOR."

"I LIKE OLDER WOMEN."

HOWEVER, I THINK I REMEMBER SHERTAIN KEY WORDSH...

GLOOOOM

......

NOT AT ALL... I WASH MERELY ENJOYING MY FREE DRINKSH.

SO...⇒HIC⇐ DIDJA GET WHAT HE WASH TALKIN' ABOUT?

⇒HIC⇐

CLINK CLINK

210

*HMM.*

PERHAPS HE MERELY WISHED TO HAVE THIS INFORMATION PASSED ON TO YOU.

OKAY, SO THIS... THIS *"AYAKO"* PERSON IS MARRIED AND WORKS AT A MASSAGE PARLOR. SO WHAT'S THE POINT HERE?

*SO?! SO WHAT?!*

I DUNNO... HE DID SAY HE WASN'T LIVING WITH HER OF HIS OWN FREE WILL, OR SOMETHING.

YEAH... MAYBE HE'S JUST KINDA RUBBING YOUR NOSE IN IT 'CAUSE YOU REJECTED HIM?

WHAT ARROGANCE— AS IF SHE'S BEGGING HIM TO STAY.

AT LEAST OUR STORY WAS INTERNALLY CONSISTENT.

WELL... I DON'T THINK SO.

WE DIDN'T LIE, DID WE?

*SLAM*

THAT... *THAT'S ENOUGH!*

I DON'T WANT TO HEAR ANOTHER WORD!

UMM... I WAS WONDERING IF YOU'D TALKED TO MR. YOTSUYA YET...?

HELLO, KYOKO SPEAKING...

HI, KYOKO? THIS IS YUSAKU.

RRIINNGG

I NOW UNDERSTAND YOUR CURRENT SITUATION QUITE THOROUGHLY.

SO...UH... WHEN CAN I MOVE BACK?

Y-YOU DO? THAT'S GREAT!

YES, I HAVE.

ffh

WHAM!!

UNFORTUNATELY, *ALL* OF THE OPEN ROOMS HAVE BEEN RENTED!

SO... SO HOW ABOUT ROOM 2, OR NUMBER 3?

REGRETTABLY, I'VE ALREADY FOUND A NEW TENANT FOR YOUR ROOM.

OH?

I... I DON'T BELIEVE IT.

MRS. OTONASHI, ISN'T IT?

OH, HELLO!

EXCUSE ME...?

THAT... THAT LITTLE—

I NEVER WANT TO SEE HIS FACE AGAIN!

OH, NO.

IT SOUNDS AS THOUGH THE COUPLE IS TAKING ADVANTAGE OF HIS KINDNESS.

I TELL YOU, HE SEEMS TOTALLY MISERABLE.

WHAT?

SO HE'S JUST BOARDING WITH A MARRIED COUPLE?

YOU KNOW... I FIGURED THE STORY WOULDN'T MAKE IT INTACT.

I... I SEE.

NOW I'VE REALLY **DONE** IT.

WHAT A DISASTER.

SSHH

......

SSHH

*HEH...* WE KIND OF FOUND OUT THE **REAL** STORY FROM THE GUY AT CHA CHA MARU.

Y-YES...? WHAT IS IT?

EXCUSE US...

GOOD NEWS, *EH*, KYOKO?! LET'S CELEBRATE WITH A LI'L DRINKIE!

YOU KNOW, I'M REALLY HAPPY. YUSAKU *IS* AS NAÏVE AS I ALWAYS THOUGHT.

BLUP BLUP

WELL, YEAH, BUT WE WERE COMPLETELY DRUNK.

WHAT DO YOU MEAN, THE "REAL STORY"...? I THOUGHT YOU WERE ALL THERE LISTENING TO YUSAKU.

214

"UNFORTUNATELY, ALL OF THE OPEN ROOMS HAVE BEEN RENTED!"

THIS REALLY *IS* A DISASTER!

I DON'T BELIEVE IT.

IT'S GOTTA BE A JOKE.

EH?!

SSHH!

BOWF?

AW, C'MON, KYOKO!! QUIT CLEANING UP!

THAT'S SO *BORING*!!

NO, WAIT-!

SOUNDS LIKE THEY'RE HAVING A WELCOMING PARTY...

THERE'S A... A LIGHT IN MY ROOM!

THEN... THEN IT *WAS* TRUE.

THIS WAS ALL MY FAULT...

YUSAKU, PLEASE COME BACK.

*NOW* I'M REALLY ALL ALONE...

AKEMI!!

BLOOSH

PART ELEVEN
# DOWN THE HOME STRETCH

218

OH, YUSAKU...

SO... UH... WHEN CAN I MOVE BACK?

KYOKO...?

WHERE COULD HE HAVE GONE?

NOW WHAT DO I DO?

I'M SO SORRY...

YES.

IT'S GOTTEN QUITE CHILLY, LATELY.

HWOOOOO

UM... NO.

KLAKK

SO, HAVE YOU HEARD FROM YUSAKU?

I... I DON'T KNOW.

WHAT DO YOU THINK?

 I WONDER WHY HE HASN'T CONTACTED US...?

 ...... ......

 OF COURSE.

CAN I HAVE SOME MORE?

 SLRPP

 ...... KLAKK SPLSSH

I REALLY WONDER WHY YUSAKU HASN'T COME BACK...

 SSHH

W-WHAT? WHAT?

HEY, YOU!

......

LOOK, MAYBE YOU CAN FOOL THE REST OF THE WORLD, BUT I KNOW YOU BETTER THAN THAT.

ALL RIGHT, WHAT DID YOU DO?

W-WHAT DO YOU MEAN?

B... BUT...

SO WHAT HAPPENED?

C'MON, YOU CAN TELL ME.

WELL, THEN...

YOU REALLY THINK SO?

LOOK, IF I KNOW SOMETHING HAPPENED, MAYBE WE CAN DO SOMETHING ABOUT IT...

...IF WE PUT OUR HEADS TOGETHER.

B-BUT I...

W-WHAT?! YOU TOLD HIM ALL THE ROOMS WERE RENTED?!?

HEY, AKEMI, LISTEN TO **THIS!!**

MORNING.

B-BUT...

SO **THAT'S** WHY HE HASN'T COME BACK.

WHAAAT? JEEZ, KYOKO, WHAT AN AWFUL THING TO SAY!

WELL, YEAH, OKAY... TRUE.

BECAUSE... WELL, YOU **ALL** TOLD ME HE WAS BRAGGING ABOUT LIVING WITH THIS "AYAKO" PERSON.

SHIK

OH, YEAH?

IT'S PARTLY **YOUR** FAULT, TOO, AKEMI!!

YEAH... WHY SHOULD A MANAGER CARE ABOUT A TENANT'S PERSONAL LIFE, ANYWAY?

BUT...

HONESTLY, KYOKO... WHY'D YOU HAVE TO TELL HIM SUCH AN AWFUL LIE?

LET'S PUT OUR HEAD'S TOGETHER AND—

OKAY, NOW THAT YOU KNOW WHAT HAPPENED...

LOOK, THIS ISN'T THE TIME FOR SUCH NONSENSE!

SURE DOES.

Y'KNOW... THIS LOOKS LIKE A LOVER'S SPAT, DOESN'T IT?

BUT DON'T YOU FEEL BETTER HAVING GOTTEN IT OFF YOUR CHEST?

HERE I TOLD YOU EVERYTHING, AND NOW YOU JUST—

BUT...

FORGET IT— THIS LOOKS PRETTY HOPELESS TO ME.

*WHY* DID I EVEN OPEN MY MOUTH?!

**SLAM**

YEAH, MAYBE WE JUST BETTER FORGET ABOUT HIM.

223

WATCH WHERE YOU'RE GOING, IDIOT!

BMP

WHAT IF HE GETS DESPERATE AND...

ASK ME IF I CARE, YOU GODDAMN JERK!

SNIK

HEY, PAL... YOU DISRE-SPECTIN' ME?

HYAAAR GGH!

THEN DIE, PUNK!

HWOOOOO

N-NO... NOT THAT!

K... KYOKO...

TWIST TWIST

224

=SNIFF=
=SNORK=

HAA-
CHOO!!

MAN, YOU ARE SICK AS A DOG.

=SNIFF=

BLOSH

OF COURSE I GOT A COLD...

...IT WAS FREEZING COLD THAT NIGHT.

HA-CHOO!

KANG KANG

HYOOOO

226

NO...

...THERE ARE NO ROOMS LEFT.

YOU SURE YOU CAN'T JUST GO BACK TO MAISON IKKOKU?

IT WAS ALL MY OWN DAMN FAULT TO BEGIN WITH.

ANYWAY, I'M SURE TO FIND A PLACE IN A COUPLE OF DAYS.

-SNURK-

YEAH, AND THE MANAGER'S KINDA A COLD FISH, TOO, HUH?

AW, SHUDDAP

I DUNNO, SAKAMOTO... I'VE ALREADY BEEN HERE A WEEK.

WELL, DON'T WORRY – YOU CAN CAMP OUT HERE UNTIL THEN.

YOU'RE A PAL.

WELL, OKAY.

-SZNXX-

YEAH, BUT I REALLY SHOULDN'T...

FORGET IT, I SAID.

YUSAKU GODAI?

KYOKO HERE. *UMM...* IS YUSAKU THERE?

TODAY'S THE DAY HE TUTORS IKUKO, RIGHT?

HELLO, MR. OTONASHI...?

HIS VOICE SOUNDED TERRIBLE.

WELL, DEAR, HE CALLED IN TO CANCEL – SAID HE HAD A BAD COLD.

N-NO... FORGET IT. THANKS, MR. OTONASHI.

DID SOMETHING HAPPEN TO HIM?

HE SOUNDED LIKE HE WAS AT DEATH'S DOOR, IN MY OPINION.

ISN'T HE THERE?

HE... HE'S REALLY SICK?

KOFF KOFF

HWOOOO

KLIK

I WONDER WHY...?

SICK...

KANGG

K... KYOKO...

KOFF KOFF KOFF

KOFF STAGGER

WHOO

HWOOOOO

N-NO... NOT THAT!

...SO I COULD APOLOGIZE.

IF I COULD ONLY SEE HIM JUST ONCE MORE...

HOW COME THINGS HAD TO TURN OUT LIKE THIS?

WURF BOWF

MR. SOICHIRO, WHAT SHOULD I DO...?

HOW *COULD* I HAVE SAID SUCH THINGS TO HIM?

BUT HE'LL PROBABLY NEVER CALL AGAIN.

SNZZ GZNZZ

I CAN'T REALLY EXPECT MOM AND DAD TO HELP ME OUT OF THIS ONE, EITHER.

FIRST, I GOTTA FIND A NEW PART-TIME JOB.

-SNFF-

HWOOO

I CAN HARDLY AFFORD ANYTHING ...

-SNRRK-

東京不動産

FWMP WHUD KSSH

?

NOK NOK

-SNRFF-

YO, SAKA-MOTO!

LEMME IN.

230

TUMP
TUMP
TUMP

NOK
NOK

SAKAMOTO

HWOOOO

HA-
CHOO!

OH.
"GIRL-
FRIEND,"
HUH?

:SNFF:

TOIK

WHAT'S
UP?

GEE,
YOU'RE
EARLY.

CHAK

UH,
HI.

JUST
TAKE
YOUR
TIME,
OKAY?

THANKS
FOR
LETTING
ME
STAY.

I'VE
GOT
ANOTHER
PLACE
TO GO.

SORRY,
YUSAKU, BUT
YOU MIND
CATCHING A
MOVIE OR
SOMETHING?

SAKAMOTO

HEY,
HEY, NO
PROBLEM.

HAA-
CHOO!!

HWOOOOO

DAMN... NOT ENOUGH MONEY!

UH-OH!

GUESS I MAY AS WELL JUST GO TO AN ALL-NIGHT MOVIE...

OH, WELL...

HWOOO

BRRRRR

HWOOOOOO

HWOOOO

YOU REALLY DON'T HAVE A PLACE FOR ME ANYMORE, KYOKO...?

KYOKO...

INDEED. THE ENTIRE PURPOSE OF OUR INVITATION WAS TO ATTEMPT TO RAISE YOUR SPIRITS.

YOU'LL FEEL BETTER IF YOU HAVE ONE.

COME ON, KYOKO – HAVE A DRINK.

PERSONALLY, I FIGURE THE WHOLE BUNCH OF YOU ARE GUILTY.

OH, YEAH?

IT WASN'T REALLY *ANYBODY'S* FAULT.

LOOK, MOPING WON'T HELP ANYTHING.

BOWF?

HWOOOOOO

IF I DRINK, I'LL JUST START CRYING...

I SHOULDN'T.

THAT'S A GOOD BOY!

SEEMS LIKE YOU REMEMBER ME, HUH?

HEY, MR. SOICHIRO.

BOWF BOWF

FFT FFT

LOOKS LIKE EVERYONE'S OUT...

-:HIC:-

DESPITE YOUR PROTEST-ATIONS, YOU CERTAINLY CONSUMED A GREAT DEAL OF ALCOHOL.

ARE YOU OKAY, KYOKO?

...EVEN THOUGH IT ISN'T REALLY HOME ANYMORE.

MY FEET JUST TOOK ME HERE...

BOWF!

WHSSK

EEP!

HEY, YOU! WHAT ARE YOU UP TO?

A BURGLAR, ISN'T IT?!

THAT'S ...

HOLD IT RIGHT THERE! HELP, THIEF!

THMP

YU...

PLEASE STOP!

YUSAKU!

KYOKO, DON'T!!

THMP THMP THMP

GO AWAY!

WAIT!!

D-DID SHE SAY "YUSAKU"...?

I DON'T WANT TO LIVE WITH YOU ANYMORE!!

I SAID LEAVE ME ALONE!!

I WILL NOT!!

YOU STOP *RIGHT* NOW!

BUT THAT'S WHAT I—

VWHIP

YUSAKU GODAI!!

-SNFF-
-SNRK-

YEAH... WHY *AM* I RUNNING AWAY, ANYHOW?

DON'T YOU *DARE* RUN AWAY FROM ME!!

237

HUFF
HUFF

HAHH
HAHH

-SNURFF-

-SNFF-

OH,
YUSAKU,
*PLEASE*
COME
BACK!

K...
KYOKO...

WAAHH!

EEP!

.....

I'VE
GOT...

I'VE
GOT
ROOMS
...

......

D-DON'T C-CRY! -SNFF- PLEASE DON'T CRY!

AAHUH-HUH!

WAAAHHH!

EEP!

HWOOOOO

IF I'D HAD A CHOICE, I THINK I'D HAVE PREFERRED TO COME BACK HOME WITH A BIT MORE DIGNITY...

WELL, AT LEAST YOU HAVE RETURNED.

GOD, WHAT A SLOB... HERE'S A TISSUE.

-SNIFF- -SNFF-

SLSSH

CAN WE GET A MOVE ON HERE, PLEASE?

DO YOU MIND WALKING A BIT FASTER?

WHAT ARE YOU TWO DOING?!

C'MON, LET'S GO HOME.

# MAISON IKKOKU

VOLUME 4
Story and Art by Rumiko Takahashi

Translation/Gerard Jones & Matt Thorn
Touch-up & Lettering/Susan Daigle-Leach
Design/Nozomi Akashi
Editors-1st Edition/Satoru Fujii & Trish Ledoux
Editor-2nd Edition/Elizabeth Kawasaki

Managing Editor/Annette Roman
Editor-in-Chief/William Flanagan
Production Manager/Noboru Watanabe
Sr. Director of Licensing & Acquisitions/Rika Inouye
V.P. of Marketing/Liza Coppola
Sr. V.P. of Editorial/Hyoe Narita
Publisher/Seiji Horibuchi

Printed in Canada

Published by VIZ, LLC
P.O. Box 77010
San Francisco, CA 94107

Editor's Choice Edition
10 9 8 7 6 5 4 3 2 1

First printing, March 2004
First English edition published 1995

www.viz.com

## ABOUT THE ARTIST

Rumiko Takahashi, born in 1957 in Niigata, Japan, is the acclaimed creator and artist of *Maison Ikkoku, InuYasha, Ranma 1/2* and *Lum * Urusei Yatsura*.

She lived in a small student's apartment in Nakano, Japan, which was the basis for the *Maison Ikkoku* series, while she attended the prestigious Nihon Joseidai (Japan Women's University). At the same time, Takahashi also began studying comics at Gekiga Sonjuku, a famous school for manga artists run by Kazuo Koike, author of *Crying Freeman* and *Lone Wolf and Cub*. In 1978, Takahashi won a prize in Shogakukan's annual New Comic Artist Contest and her boy-meets-alien comedy *Lum * Urusei Yatsura* began appearing in the weekly manga magazine *Shonen Sunday*.

Takahashi's success and critical acclaim continues to grow, with popular titles including *Ranma 1/2* and *InuYasha*. Many of her graphic novel series have also been animated, and are widely available in several languages.

# EDITOR'S RECOMMENDATIONS

**More manga!**
**More manga!**

Fans of

# maison ikkoku

should also read:

©1988 Rumiko
Takahashi/Shogakukan Inc.

### RANMA 1/2

Rumiko Takahashi's gender-bending comedy series is the tale of a father and son who fall into cursed springs in China, and their lives are transformed, literally. When they get wet, the father turns into a panda and the son, Ranma, turns into a girl. Comic situations ensue as they try and keep their friends and family, especially Ranma's fiancé and her family, from finding out their secret.

©1992 YOKO
KAMINO/SHUEISHA Inc.

### BOYS OVER FLOWERS

Makino Tsukushi and her friend Makiko Yuki are cute, popular high school girls. But their lives change for the worse when a gang of rich boys influences the entire school to taunt them. Finally, this extremely popular shôjo series makes it debut in the U.S.

© 1997 Tokihiko
Matsuura/Shogakukan, Inc.

### TUXEDO GIN

In Tokihiko Matsuura's romantic comedy, 17-year-old Ginji Kusanagi meets the girl of his dreams, Minako Sasebo, but is killed in an accident before they go on their first date. Ginji is reincarnated as a penguin, and Minako adopts him as her pet, but she has no idea that he's actually her dearly departed love.

# INUYASHA™

Rated #1 on Cartoon Network's Adult Swim!

In its original unedited form.

# maison ikkoku™

The beloved romantic comedy of errors—a fan favorite!

# Ranma ½™

The zany, wacky study of martial arts at its best!

# COMPLETE OUR SURVEY AND LET US KNOW WHAT YOU THINK!

☐ Please check here if you DO NOT wish to receive information or future offers from VIZ

Name: _____

Address: _____

City: _____ State: _____ Zip: _____

E-mail: _____

☐ Male ☐ Female   Date of Birth (mm/dd/yyyy): ___/___/___   ( Under 13? Parental consent required )

## What race/ethnicity do you consider yourself? (please check one)

☐ Asian/Pacific Islander        ☐ Black/African American   ☐ Hispanic/Latino

☐ Native American/Alaskan Native   ☐ White/Caucasian        ☐ Other: _____

## What VIZ product did you purchase? (check all that apply and indicate title purchased)

☐ DVD/VHS _____

☐ Graphic Novel _____

☐ Magazines _____

☐ Merchandise _____

## Reason for purchase: (check all that apply)

☐ Special offer           ☐ Favorite title          ☐ Gift

☐ Recommendation          ☐ Other_____

## Where did you make your purchase? (please check one)

☐ Comic store             ☐ Bookstore               ☐ Mass/Grocery Store

☐ Newsstand               ☐ Video/Video Game Store  ☐ Other: _____

☐ Online (site: _____ )

## What other VIZ properties have you purchased/own? _____

_____

**How many anime and/or manga titles have you purchased in the last year? How many were VIZ titles?** (please check one from each column)

| ANIME | MANGA | VIZ |
|-------|-------|-----|
| ☐ None | ☐ None | ☐ None |
| ☐ 1-4 | ☐ 1-4 | ☐ 1-4 |
| ☐ 5-10 | ☐ 5-10 | ☐ 5-10 |
| ☐ 11+ | ☐ 11+ | ☐ 11+ |

**I find the pricing of VIZ products to be:** (please check one)

☐ Cheap          ☐ Reasonable          ☐ Expensive

**What genre of manga and anime would you like to see from VIZ?** (please check two)

☐ Adventure          ☐ Comic Strip          ☐ Science Fiction          ☐ Fighting

☐ Horror          ☐ Romance          ☐ Fantasy          ☐ Sports

**What do you think of VIZ's new look?**

☐ Love It          ☐ It's OK          ☐ Hate It          ☐ Didn't Notice          ☐ No Opinion

**Which do you prefer?** (please check one)

☐ Reading right-to-left

☐ Reading left-to-right

**Which do you prefer?** (please check one)

☐ Sound effects in English

☐ Sound effects in Japanese with English captions

☐ Sound effects in Japanese only with a glossary at the back

**THANK YOU! Please send the completed form to:**

NJW Research
42 Catharine St.
Poughkeepsie, NY 12601